MENINGITIS

MENINGITIS

CONNIE GOLDSMITH

Twenty-First Century Medical Library

TF
CB

Twenty-First Century Books
Minneapolis

The images in this book are used with the permission of: © Medioimages/Getty Images, pp. 3, 7, 10, 20, 36, 50, 64, 82, 98; © Dr. Dennis Kunkel/Visuals Unlimited, p. 9; Library of Congress (LC-DIG-ggbain-12475), p. 11; © Bettmann/ CORBIS, p. 13; Centers for Disease and Control and Prevention Public Health Image Library, pp. 16, 58; © Nucleus Medical Art/Visuals Unlimited, p. 24; © WoodyStock/Alamy, p. 44; © Dr. Fred Hossler/Visuals Unlimited, p. 56; © Arthur Siegelman/Visuals Unlimited, p. 57; Centers for Disease and Control and Prevention Public Health Image Library/Maryam I. Daneshvar, Ph.D., p. 71; AP Photo/Brian Branch-Price, p. 73; AP Photo, p. 75; AP Photo/Ng Han Guan, p. 80; AP Photo/David J. Phillip, p. 87; © Barry Slaven/Visuals Unlimited, p. 89; © Tek Image/Photo Researchers, Inc., p. 92; © Science VU/CDC/Visuals Unlimited, p. 101; © Science VU/Wellcome/Visuals Unlimited, p. 102.

Front cover: © Dr. Dennis Kunkel/Visuals Unlimited (left); © Medioimages/ Getty Images (right)

Dedicated to every family that has been touched by meningitis, and with special thanks to my writing partners, Erin Dealey and Patricia M. Newman, for their endless support and encouragement.

Twenty-First Century Books
A division of Lerner Publishing Group, Inc.
241 First Avenue North
Minneapolis, MN 55401 U.S.A.

Website address: www.lernerbooks.com

Library of Congress Cataloging-in-Publication Data

Goldsmith, Connie, 1945–
    Meningitis / by Connie Goldsmith.
        p.   cm. — (Twenty-first century medical library)
    Includes bibliographical references and index.
    ISBN 978–0–8225–7034–9 (lib. bdg. : alk. paper)
    1. Meningitis—Juvenile literature. I. Title.
RC376.G65 2008
616.8'2—dc22   2007003185

Manufactured in the United States of America
1 2 3 4 5 6 – BP – 13 12 11 10 09 08

CONTENTS

INTRODUCTION

Meningitis in the Headlines

Duluth, Minnesota: Seventh-grade boy hospitalized with meningitis

Los Angeles, California: Child and college student die of a rare and virulent form of meningococcal meningitis

Indianapolis, Indiana: 18-year-old freshman at Indiana University recovering after bacterial meningitis

Ambler, Pennsylvania: 70 children taking antibiotics after day-care worker diagnosed with meningitis

Eudora, Kansas: Doctors diagnose meningitis caused by West Nile virus in teen boy

Portland, Oregon: Three-year-old girl dies of bacterial meningitis two and a half hours after being admitted to Children's Hospital

Baltimore, Maryland: 19-year-old sophomore at Johns Hopkins University diagnosed with bacterial meningitis

Pikeville, Kentucky: 15-year-old granddaughter of former governor's wife found dead of meningitis on Christmas morning

Atlanta, Georgia: 7th grader hospitalized with bacterial meningitis. Parents at the middle school are advised to watch their children for signs of illness

These recent newspaper headlines tell about a few of the thousands of people who get a disease called meningitis each year. Meningitis is an infection of the meninges, the paper-thin membranes that cover and protect the brain and spinal cord. While meningitis can strike anyone, it is most common in children, teens, and young adults. Meningitis strikes fear into the hearts of parents and health-care workers because it often affects the youngest and most vulnerable people.

Meningitis can cause a long list of symptoms. But it is best known for its "triad" of symptoms—fever, stiff neck, and impaired level of consciousness (such as confusion, fatigue, and irritability). Most people recover from meningitis. A few others are left with serious permanent problems, such as speech and learning disabilities, brain damage, deafness, or loss of fingers, toes, hands, and feet. Even with the best medical care, some forms of meningitis kill one or two out of every ten people who get it.

Meningitis is different from a disease such as Lyme disease, in which only one kind of bacterium is the culprit. Meningitis can be caused by many kinds of dangerous

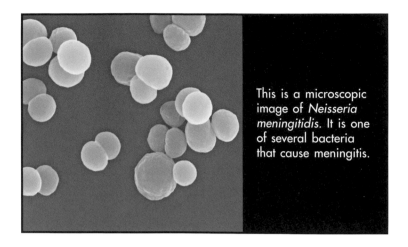

This is a microscopic image of *Neisseria meningitidis*. It is one of several bacteria that cause meningitis.

microorganisms (living organisms so small that you need a microscope to see them). These microorganisms include bacteria, viruses, and fungi. The most dangerous type of bacterial meningitis may kill people within twenty-four hours after they start feeling sick. People with meningitis caused by viruses usually are not as sick as those with bacterial meningitis. However, both types require prompt medical attention because only a doctor can tell the difference.

Health care has made great strides over the past twenty years in the prevention and treatment of meningitis. Even though some forms of meningitis can be prevented with vaccination, it's important to learn about meningitis so you can help protect yourself, your family, and your friends from this terrible disease. While meningitis is not as contagious (easily spread among people) as a cold or the flu, it can be passed by something as simple as sharing a cookie, a Coke, or a kiss.

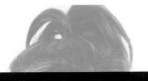

MENINGITIS—PAST AND PRESENT

Helen Keller

Born in 1880 in Alabama, Helen Keller was a happy and lively child until she was nineteen months old. Then she was struck with a terrible illness that left her permanently blind and deaf. We can only imagine how devastated her parents must have been. Their little girl seemed destined to live forever in a dark and silent world.

But Helen Keller went on to have a remarkable life. She learned to speak, read, and write with the help of her dedicated teacher, Anne Sullivan. Helen Keller overcame her disabilities and graduated from Radcliffe College in Massachusetts. She went on to become a world-famous lecturer and advocate for the disabled. Books, plays, and even a movie (The Miracle Worker) have been written

Helen Keller may have lost her sight and hearing to meningitis.

about her. While modern medical historians cannot be certain, they believe the disease that robbed Keller of her hearing and her sight was meningitis.

Scientists believe that meningitis has been around for centuries. The common signs of meningitis—fever, neck stiffness, confusion, rash, and headache—were described in the Middle Ages (the years between about A.D. 600–1450). Doctors first identified bacterial meningitis as a specific disease during an outbreak in Switzerland in 1805. But they didn't yet know what caused it.

By the end of the nineteenth century, microscopes had improved. They were strong enough to allow doctors to identify many kinds of bacteria, including those that cause meningitis. In 1887 German doctor Anton Weichselbaum identified meningococcus—the bacterium responsible for the most dangerous kind of meningitis. Weichselbaum examined people known to have meningococcal meningitis. He took samples of their cerebrospinal fluid (CSF—the clear liquid that circulates in the brain, meninges, and spinal canal). After isolating the bacterium, Weichselbaum grew more in a laboratory. Then he injected animals with the bacteria. When the animals developed meningococcal meningitis, it proved that the bacterium he had identified was indeed the culprit.

Researchers didn't discover the viruses that cause meningitis until several decades later. Viruses are too small to be seen through regular microscopes, so scientists couldn't identify them until after the invention of the electron microscope in the 1930s. Modern medicine knows of more than a dozen different organisms that can cause meningitis.

MENINGITIS VICTIMS

In 1792 the Spanish painter Francisco de Goya came down with what is believed to have been meningitis. Even though it left him completely deaf, he was one of the lucky ones. At the time, nearly everyone who got meningitis died.

Brain fever and spotted fever were early names for what was likely meningitis. Brain fever was common enough into the nineteenth century that writers Charles Dickens, Mark Twain, and Sir Arthur Conan Doyle mentioned it in their stories.

One of the most famous people to die from confirmed meningitis was Oscar Wilde, the Irish-born playwright (*The Importance of Being Earnest*) and novelist (*The Picture of Dorian Gray*). Wilde's plays and books were popular, and he was a famous social figure in London. He died of meningitis in 1900 at the age of forty-six while living in Paris.

Meningitis was once called the "disease of children and soldiers" because it was so common in those groups of people. Young children are always more susceptible to infectious diseases of all kinds. Their immune systems (the parts of the body that work to identify and fight disease-causing organisms such as bacteria and viruses) have not yet matured enough to easily fight off infections.

Outbreaks of meningitis have plagued the military for decades. Meningitis spreads much more quickly in the crowded conditions where troops live and work. So many British troops developed meningitis during World War I (1914–1918), that doctors studied exactly how far apart bunks should be placed in order to reduce spread of the disease by coughing or sneezing.

Meningitis outbreaks hit U.S. troops hard during World War I, World War II (1939–1945), the Korean War

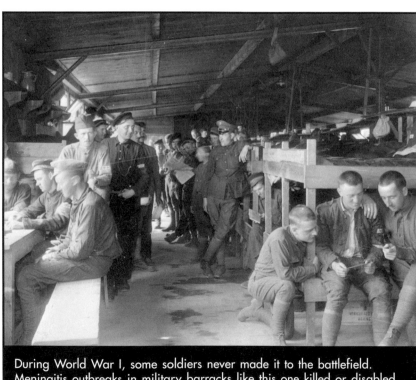

During World War I, some soldiers never made it to the battlefield. Meningitis outbreaks in military barracks like this one killed or disabled many people because there were few effective treatments for it.

(1950–1953), and the Vietnam War (1965–1973). Currently, new recruits in the U.S. military are required to be vaccinated against meningitis, so far fewer cases occur.

MENINGITIS IN THE UNITED STATES

Health officials can count the number of people who get a disease only if the cases are reported to a central registry. In the United States, the central registry is the Centers for Disease Control and Prevention (CDC), headquartered in Atlanta, Georgia. This government agency is responsible for collecting information about health conditions and infectious diseases across the United States. By law, doctors must report certain diseases to the CDC—for example, all cases of meningitis caused by meningococcal bacteria. Approximately 17,500 Americans develop bacterial meningitis each year. That doesn't seem like a lot of people, but meningitis caused by bacteria is always considered a life-threatening illness.

Doctors are not required to report cases of meningitis caused by viruses to the CDC. However, hospitals keep records about why people are admitted. Health officials collect this information and use it to determine how many people are hospitalized for viral meningitis and other conditions. Those records show that an estimated 50,000 people each year end up in hospitals with viral meningitis. Many other people with milder cases of viral meningitis are treated in their doctors' offices or at home, and so are not counted. Some estimates put the total number of Americans who get viral meningitis each year at 75,000 or more.

MENINGITIS AROUND THE WORLD

Worldwide, infectious diseases of every kind kill about 1,500 people each hour. Half of those people are children under five years old. World health officials estimate that 9 out of 10 deaths caused by infections are due to these diseases: respiratory infections, HIV/AIDS, diseases that cause diarrhea, tuberculosis, malaria, measles, pertussis (whooping cough), tetanus, and meningitis.

Meningitis occurs in every country around the world. You might expect that large numbers of meningitis cases occur primarily in poor countries, and you'd be right. Yet meningitis strikes even in wealthy, industrialized nations. For example, New Zealand, England, Scotland, and Ireland all have higher rates of meningitis than the United States does.

But no region suffers more from meningitis than does Africa. So many people in Africa get meningitis that a section of the country has been dubbed the "meningitis belt." This vast area touches twenty-one countries from Senegal and Gambia in the west, through Mali, Niger, Chad, and Sudan in the center of Africa, to Ethiopia in the east. Nearly 400 million people live in or near the meningitis belt. Other areas of Africa also experience significant numbers of meningitis cases.

Major meningitis epidemics (widespread outbreaks) have taken place in the African meningitis belt for the past one hundred years. The major outbreaks seem to occur every eight to twelve years. In other years, smaller outbreaks peak in the dry season, which in Africa is December through June. The cool nights and swirling sand storms common in those months lead to an increase in the upper respiratory infections that often precede meningitis. Sand and infections irritate and weaken the protective mechanisms of the lining of the nose and throat. This allows bacteria to more easily enter the body.

Extreme poverty also contributes to the spread of meningitis in Africa. Poverty-stricken people usually have poor nutrition and generally weakened immune systems. The crowded living conditions in family homes and refugee camps also increase the chance of meningitis outbreaks and numerous other diseases.

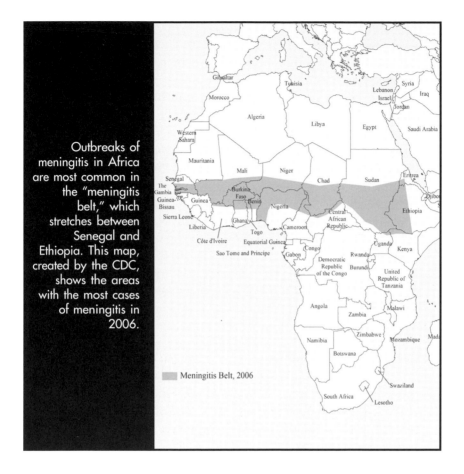

Outbreaks of meningitis in Africa are most common in the "meningitis belt," which stretches between Senegal and Ethiopia. This map, created by the CDC, shows the areas with the most cases of meningitis in 2006.

Meningitis Belt, 2006

Meningococcal bacteria are the only bacteria known to cause epidemics of meningitis. For example, nearly 700,000 people in the meningitis belt developed meningococcal meningitis during the ten-year period from 1995 to 2004. Sixty thousand of those people died.

The largest recorded outbreak of meningococcal meningitis in history occurred in Africa's meningitis belt during 1996. In just one year, more than 250,000 people, mainly children and teens, came down with the disease. At least 25,000 of them died. In some villages, as many as 1 out of every 100 people developed meningitis. For comparison, only 1 or 2 people out of every 100,000 people in the United States develop the same kind of meningitis.

Two other kinds of bacterial meningitis that occur throughout Africa may kill between 250,000 and 500,000 children per year. Many of these deaths could be prevented by available vaccines. However, most people living in this region cannot afford even the most basic medical care, much less expensive vaccines.

Combined with the burden of other infectious diseases such as AIDS, malaria, and tuberculosis, meningitis adds to the ongoing poverty of the African continent. Sick adults cannot work, tend their animals, or grow their crops. Sick children cannot attend school or help out with household chores. These conditions can weaken entire societies.

Planning a Trip?

Vaccines can prevent several kinds of bacterial meningitis. People planning to travel outside the United States should talk to their doctors or county health departments to see if a meningitis vaccination is recommended for the destination country. The CDC advises Americans who plan to visit Africa's meningitis belt during the dry season to be vaccinated against meningococcal meningitis several weeks before they plan to travel.

Saudi Arabia is the only country with a requirement for meningitis vaccination. In 1987, there was a serious outbreak of bacterial meningitis among Muslims making their hajj (a religious pilgrimage) to the city of Mecca in Saudi Arabia. Nearly 2 million Muslims from around the world make a hajj to Mecca each year. So the potential for further outbreaks remains high. Since the 1987 outbreak, Saudi health authorities require hajj pilgrims to get meningitis vaccinations prior to entering the country.

ANATOMY OF A MENINGITIS EPIDEMIC

In 1974 the CDC sent Dr. Joe McCormick, a specialist in tropical medicine, to Brazil to help out with an epidemic of bacterial meningitis. McCormick arrived at a large hospital overflowing with sick and dying people, most of them children, teens, and young adults. In some Brazilian hospitals, 3 out of 4 infants and 6 out of 10 adults with meningitis died during the epidemic.

McCormick worked with Brazilian health authorities to identify factors causing the epidemic. He noted that most of the meningitis victims came from the poorest regions of the largest cities, such as Rio de Janeiro and São Paolo. In these urban districts, people live in conditions of extreme poverty in crowded tin shacks without clean running water.

Doctors discovered that two strains of meningitis were circulating. At the time, meningitis vaccines were experimental and had not been used on large numbers of people. A French drug company quickly developed a new vaccine to protect against both strains.

Early in 1975, more than 3 million people in Rio de Janeiro were vaccinated against meningitis. In April 1975, in perhaps the largest vaccination campaign in history, the Brazilian government vaccinated 11 million residents of São Paulo against meningitis in just four days.

Ultimately, 80 million Brazilians were vaccinated, but not before meningitis had sickened 250,000 people and killed 11,000 of them. Nearly one-third of the survivors were left with serious physical damage, such as deafness or brain damage.

Anyone planning an overseas trip can contact the CDC for information about required vaccinations prior to departure. The CDC offers extensive information about travel to nearly any country. The CDC's *Travelers' Health: Yellow Book* also provides updated health information each year for world travelers (available by mail or on the CDC website). The World Health Organization (WHO) offers a booklet with similar information titled, *International Travel and Health*.

Chapter 2

MENINGITIS BASICS

Jack's Story

Like Helen Keller, Jack was not even two years old when he came down with meningitis. Even though Jack had been treated for five ear infections during his short life, he seemed pretty healthy. One day when Jack's mom picked him up from day care, she discovered the toddler had a fever. She took him to the doctor, who diagnosed yet another ear infection. The doctor told Jack's mom to treat the fever with Tylenol, and he gave her another pre-scription for a new antibiotic.

The next day—a Saturday—Jack seemed to feel a lot better. His fever was down and his dad took him to the park to play. Jack's parents breathed a sigh of relief. It looked like he would get over this ear infection, just like he'd gotten over

the others. On Sunday morning, Jack's mom dis-
covered that his fever was back. The little boy was
drowsy and wouldn't wake up. Jack's worried par-
ents took him to the emergency room (ER) where
the doctors diagnosed him with meningitis.

Before we can understand what happened when Jack came down with meningitis, we need to know a little about the central nervous system. The central nervous system is our body's command center. It is made up of the brain, the twelve sets of cranial nerves that originate in the brain, the spinal cord, and the three meninges. Meningitis is an infection and inflammation (swelling) of the surface of the brain and the meninges. The meninges help to protect the delicate brain and spinal cord from injury. Starting from the brain and going outward, the meninges are:

- Pia mater (Latin for "soft mother"): The inner-most of the meninges hugs the brain and spinal cord as closely as shrink-wrapping. The pia mater is composed of blood vessels held in place by fragile tissue. It dips deep into every fissure and crevice of the brain and clings closely to the spinal cord as it travels down the back.
- Arachnoid (Latin meaning like a spider web): The middle layer of the meninges is thin and delicate. It looks somewhat like a spider web. The arachnoid is composed of bundles of white rubbery tissue. It lies loosely over the pia mater. The space between the pia and arachnoid layers is called the subarachnoid space.
- Dura mater (Latin for "tough mother"): The outermost of the meninges is a strong, tough membrane. It lines the inside of the skull and continues all the way down the spine to the coc-cyx, or tailbone. The dura mater surrounds and protects the spinal cord and the brain.

21

CRANIAL NERVES

Twelve pairs of cranial nerves arise from the brain, unlike other nerves in the body, which branch off from the spinal cord. Meningitis may damage the cranial nerves, explaining why some victims are left with hearing or vision problems. Any of the cranial nerves can be affected, but the eighth (VIII) is the one most often damaged by meningitis. Note that cranial nerves are always written in Roman numerals.

#	Name of nerve	Function
I	Olfactory	Smell
II	Optic	Vision
III	Oculomotor	Eye movement and pupil dilation
IV	Trochlear	Eye movement
V	Trigeminal	Chewing muscles and sensation of the face and head
VI	Abducens	Eye movement
VII	Facial	Taste in the front part of the tongue, sensation around the ear area, and muscles used to make facial expressions
VIII	Vestibulocochlear	Hearing and balance
IX	Glossopharyngeal	Taste in the back part of the tongue; sensation in the tongue, tonsils, and throat; some muscles used in swallowing
X	Vagus	Controls movement and automatic functions of some organs (for example, heart rate and digestion)
XI	Spinal accessory	Muscles used in head movement
XII	Hypoglossal	Muscles of the tongue

The clear liquid called the cerebrospinal fluid (CSF) is continually formed in the brain. CSF circulates through the brain and flows in the subarachnoid space and up and down the spinal canal (the space through which the spinal cord passes). Along with the bones of the spine and skull, CSF protects the brain and spinal cord. Try an experiment to see for yourself how CSF works. Smack yourself on the thigh. Ouch! Then, the next time you're in a swimming pool, try the same thing underwater. The water slows the speed and force of your hand so much that you barely feel the slap.

CSF is like the pool water. When you bump your head, your brain is cushioned by the "sloshing" of the CSF. If you didn't have any CSF and bumped your head, your soft brain would smash against the hard inside of your skull. Ouch again! If that happened, you'd get a concussion, sort of like a big bruise on the brain. Worse yet, the blood vessels in and around your brain could tear and bleed, leading to serious or even fatal brain damage.

Meningitis occurs when bacteria, viruses, or other microorganisms get into the CSF. Microorganisms can enter the CSF in a number of ways. CSF then carries the infectious organisms throughout the meninges.

Our blood is filled with white blood cells and antibodies (substances produced by the immune system to help our bodies fight specific infections). An organism that invades the blood is quickly met with an army of protective white blood cells and antibodies. But CSF normally contains few white blood cells or antibodies. Without that protection, bacteria and viruses can rapidly multiply in the CSF once they get in. It doesn't take long before someone with meningitis becomes very sick.

You may have heard the term "spinal meningitis." That is not an accurate description of meningitis. The meninges cover the brain and the spinal cord, and CSF circulates around both. An infection of the meninges cannot be limited only to the spine. It always includes an infection of the meninges around the brain as well.

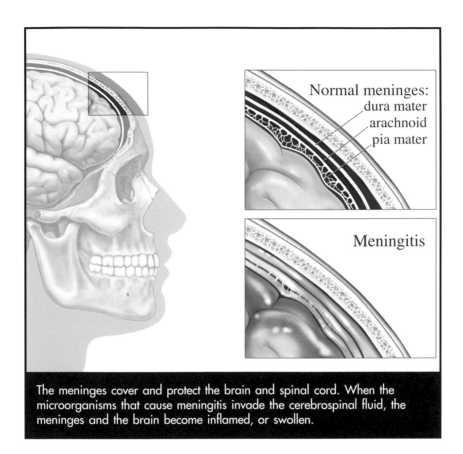

Normal meninges:
dura mater
arachnoid
pia mater

Meningitis

The meninges cover and protect the brain and spinal cord. When the microorganisms that cause meningitis invade the cerebrospinal fluid, the meninges and the brain become inflamed, or swollen.

GETTING TO KNOW BACTERIA AND VIRUSES

A number of microorganisms are known to cause meningitis. However, bacteria and viruses cause most cases of meningitis. It's helpful to know a little bit about bacteria and viruses in general before learning about the ones that can cause meningitis.

Bacteria

Bacteria are prokaryotes—single-celled microorganisms whose cells have no nucleus. ("Prokaryote" means "before nucleus.") They are neither plants nor animals.

Plant and animal cells have a nucleus—a large circular structure inside the cell. Inside the nucleus are the chromosomes, stringlike structures made up of DNA (deoxyribonucleic acid—the hereditary material that determines the development and characteristics of every organism). Bacteria don't have nuclei. Instead, their DNA freely floats within the cells, usually in a loop or coil. Bacteria cells have sturdy walls called capsules, which are formed of compounds of sugar and protein (large complex molecules).

Most bacteria can be seen with a good microscope. Scientists classify them based on their shapes:

- spherical or round (coccus)
- rodlike (bacillus)
- curving and spiraling (spirillum and spirochete)

Sometimes the name gives a hint about the bacterium's shape. For example, the bacterium *Streptococcus pneumoniae*, which causes one kind of meningitis, is round. Some bacteria have flagella—tail-like projections that propel them. Others have pili—hairlike projections that allow the bacteria to attach to cells in order to more easily invade them. Many bacteria travel with the flow of fluids, such as blood, water, and CSF.

Bacteria may be the most ancient life-form on Earth. Imprints of bacteria have been found in fossils estimated to be more than three billion years old. Bacteria can live just about anywhere. They live in freezing-cold Arctic ice pools, in the boiling hot springs of Yellowstone National Park, and even in the acid bubbling inside human stomachs. In fact, trillions of bacteria live in you and on you. You're probably carrying more than 5 pounds of bacteria inside your body right now! We eat them, drink them, and breathe them in every minute of every day. Most of the time, our strong immune systems prevent bacteria from making us sick.

BACTERIA OR VIRUS?

Doctors must figure out whether a bacterium or a virus is making someone sick. Antibiotics cure many bacterial infections, but they won't help viral infections. In fact, taking antibiotics for viral infections is not only useless, it gives bacteria a chance to become resistant to these important medications. Here are a few infections you probably have heard about.

Bacterial diseases
Gonorrhea
Lyme disease
Syphilis
Strep throat
Tetanus
Tuberculosis
Whooping cough

Diseases caused by bacteria and viruses
Ear, eye, sinus, and throat infections
Encephalitis
Meningitis
Pneumonia

Viral diseases
AIDS
Colds
Hepatitis
Influenza
SARS
West Nile

While most bacteria aren't dangerous to people, others can cause serious disease such as meningitis. Inside the human body, harmful bacteria cause damage by releasing chemical poisons called toxins. Toxins weaken and kill human cells, producing some of the symptoms of illness. These toxins are one reason why bacterial meningitis is usually so much more dangerous than meningitis caused by viruses.

Bacterial infections are especially dangerous when the bacteria invade and overwhelm the bloodstream, a condition called septicemia. While an infected cut on your finger is bothersome, a widespread infection such as septicemia is immediately life-threatening. Septicemia damages major organs such as the heart, lungs, and kidneys. Fortunately, antibiotics can cure many bacterial infections.

Viruses

Not really alive, yet not quite dead, viruses are the zombies of the microscopic world. They don't need food or water. They can't move or reproduce by themselves. They don't even need oxygen to survive. Until viruses find just the right animal or human host, they exist in a kind of suspended animation. No one is sure exactly how long viruses have been on Earth, but evidence suggests that they've been around for a very long time.

Viruses are much simpler organisms than bacteria. Viruses are made of one or more strands of genetic material. They are surrounded by protective shells made of proteins. The shells are called capsids. Some viruses also may be covered by a fatty membrane made up of lipids (fatty substances found in all organisms) and proteins, called an envelope.

Viruses are much smaller than bacteria. For example, if a single bacterium were the size of a basketball, then a virus would be the size of a marble. Millions of viruses could fit inside the period at the end of this sentence. Scientists need electron microscopes to see viruses.

Viruses have only one purpose—to invade and take over the reproductive machinery of a host (home) cell, whether it belongs to a plant, an animal, or a person. Viruses cannot move by themselves, like most bacteria can. Instead, viruses have spiky protrusions that allow them to attach to and then invade the host cell. These protrusions are made of protein and act as antigens—substances that activate the host's immune system.

Once a virus has latched onto a host cell, it enters by fusing its membrane with the cell's membrane, somewhat like two soap bubbles touching. The virus then injects its own genetic material into the host cell, forcing the cell to produce copies of the virus, similar to a copy machine running at high speed. Soon, the damaged host cell ruptures and releases thousands of new viruses, each of which moves on to infect other host cells.

Viruses enter our bodies through breaks in the skin, through mucous membranes of the mouth, nose, and genitals, and through our respiratory systems (when we breathe them in). Viruses can also enter through our blood (as when someone gets the hepatitis C virus from using a dirty hypodermic needle).

Viruses make people sick because they destroy healthy cells or cause them to malfunction. Sometimes the host body attacks its own cells to get rid of the virus infecting them. Many of the symptoms we experience with a cold or the flu—such as a fever and sore throat—are actually due to the increased activity of our immune system. Because viruses live inside host cells, antibiotics cannot reach them. That makes viral infections difficult to cure.

BACTERIAL MENINGITIS

The formal names for bacteria are always written in italicized Latin. That way, people around the world who speak different languages will recognize the bacterium's name.

Bacteria are commonly called by their first initial and second name, as in N. *meningitidis*.

Bacteria that cause most kinds of bacterial meningitis

Haemophilus influenzae, or *H. influenzae*, is one kind of bacterium. Years ago, this bacterium was incorrectly labeled as the cause of influenza. It was named for the disease it was believed to cause. (Flu is actually caused by a virus.)

Humans are the only natural host for *H. influenzae*. The bacteria live in the nose, mouth, and throat of many healthy people. The bacteria are passed by respiratory droplets, those tiny specks of mucus and saliva that we spew out when we cough and sneeze. The strain of *H. influenzae* that causes meningitis is type B, so it's known as Hib. It was once the most common cause of meningitis. But it has become much less common thanks to a widely used vaccine given to young children. Currently, Hib causes less than 10 percent of the cases of bacterial meningitis, and that's largely among unvaccinated children or older adults.

Neisseria meningitidis: About 10 percent of people normally carry N. *meningitidis* (also called meningococcus) inside their nose, mouth, and throat. Most of the time, these bacteria don't make people sick. When bacteria live harmlessly in or on people, the people are said to be colonized by the bacteria. Meningococci (the plural of meningococcus) are passed from person to person by close contact with infected saliva or nasal secretions. Even if people come into contact with meningococci, they get sick only if the bacteria leave their noses and throats and enter their bloodstreams.

When N. *meningitidis* enters the bloodstream, it becomes what is called an invasive disease. Once in the blood, the bacteria may cause meningitis or septicemia. Septicemia can be fatal in just hours. N. *meningitidis* and other bacteria commonly produce poisonous toxins as they circulate through the body. Meningococcal meningitis is the most dangerous form of bacterial meningitis and the only kind that can cause epidemics of meningitis. Vaccines can help prevent some strains of meningococcal meningitis. This bacterium causes about one-fourth of all cases of bacterial meningitis.

Streptococcus pneumoniae: S. pneumoniae, also known as pneumococcus, lives in the human nose, mouth, and throat. Like meningococci, pneumococci can be passed by close contact with infected saliva or nasal secretions, although it is somewhat less contagious. Pneumococci cause ear infections and pneumonia, as well as meningitis. It's the most common cause of meningitis in adults. Nearly half the cases of bacterial meningitis are caused by this organism.

Streptococcus agalactiae is usually called group B strep. Meningitis caused by group B strep occurs mostly in newborns. The bacteria live in the birth canal of about 25 percent of all women, and babies may become infected during delivery. Group B strep causes about 15 percent of the cases of bacterial meningitis.

Listeria monocytogenes, usually just called Listeria, is found in soil, water, the gastrointestinal tract, and in tainted food. Listeria may cause food poisoning if humans eat food contaminated with the bacteria. Infection with Listeria bacteria can cause meningitis in newborns, infants, pregnant women, and the elderly.

Other bacteria may occasionally cause meningitis. These include *Escherichia coli* (known as *E. coli*), *Staphylococcus aureus* (which cause staph infections), *Klebsiella pneumoniae* (which can also cause pneumonia), and the bacteria that cause tuberculosis, Lyme disease, and syphilis. Less than 10 percent of cases of bacterial meningitis are caused by these bacteria.

Let's check in on Jack. In the ER, the doctor performed a lumbar puncture (or spinal tap), putting a needle into Jack's spine to get a sample of CSF for testing. Right away, the doctor saw the CSF was cloudy instead of clear, a sure sign of bacterial meningitis.

Jack was airlifted to a children's hospital in a nearby city. His parents followed by car, arriving two hours after Jack had been admitted to an intensive care unit (ICU). By that time, he was having seizures and had been put on a machine called a ventilator to help him breathe. Despite intravenous antibiotics, Jack got worse. He fell into a coma—loss of consciousness due to brain injury. He could no longer respond to anything. The doctors told Jack's parents that his brain was no longer functioning.

Jack's parents had to make the hardest decision of their lives. They decided to remove their son from the ventilator. Jack's mom held him while the tubes were removed and he died in her arms a few minutes later. The final laboratory report showed that Jack's meningitis was caused by S. pneumoniae.

VIRAL MENINGITIS

Viral meningitis is much more common than bacterial meningitis. Fortunately, it is usually less serious as well. Viral meningitis is sometimes called aseptic meningitis. That means that viruses do not produce the deadly toxins that bacteria produce while they circulate in the blood. While viruses have scientific Latin names like bacteria do, they are generally lumped together in broad categories.

Viruses that cause most kinds of viral meningitis

Enteroviruses are a big group of viruses that normally live in the gastrointestinal and respiratory tracts. They are the second most common group of viruses after those that cause the common cold. About 75 percent to 90 percent of viral meningitis cases are caused by enteroviruses. These viruses can be passed by direct contact with respiratory secretions. They are more contagious than the bacteria that cause meningitis.

CAUSES OF MENINGITIS

Many different kinds of bacteria, viruses, and other organisms can cause meningitis.

Bacteria

Escherichia coli (E. coli)
Found in the gastrointestinal tract; may cause meningitis in newborns or in people with weak immune systems.

Haemophilus influenzae type B (Hib)
Found in the human nose and throat. It is currently prevented by vaccination.

Listeria monocytogenes (Listeria)
Found in soil, water, and the gastrointestinal tract. Can cause meningitis in newborns, infants, pregnant women, and the elderly.

Neisseria meningitidis (meningococcus)
Found in the human nose and throat. Causes meningococcal meningitis. Vaccines offer only partial protection.

Staphylococcus aureus (staph)
Commonly found on skin. Causes about 10 percent of adult meningitis.

Streptococcus agalactiae (group B strep, or GBS)
Found in the genital area and the gastrointestinal tract. It is the most common cause of meningitis in newborns.

Streptococcus pneumoniae (pneumococcus)
Found in the human nose and throat. It is the most common cause of bacterial meningitis. Most cases can be prevented by vaccination.

Viruses
Enteroviruses
This large group of viruses causes 75 percent to 90 percent of all cases of viral meningitis.

Flaviviruses
These viruses (West Nile and others) are carried by mosquitoes.

Herpes viruses
The second most common cause of viral meningitis.

Other viruses
HIV(the virust that causes AIDS), cytomegalovirus, adenoviruses, influenza, mumps, and measles viruses have all been shown to cause meningitis.

Fungus
Cryptococcus neoformans (crypto)
Found in soil and bird droppings. Crypto meningitis is up to seven hundred times more common in people with HIV.

Amoeba
Naegleria fowleri (Naegleria)
Found in warm freshwater. Meningitis caused by these amoeba kill up to 95 percent of victims.

Because enteroviruses also live in the intestines, infected people may carry the viruses on their hands if they don't wash properly after going to the bathroom. This could be one reason why viral meningitis is so common among young children in preschools or day care centers. Little kids aren't known for washing their hands very well.

Herpes simplex viruses (the ones that cause cold sores and genital herpes) can invade the meninges to cause meningitis. They may be the second most common cause of viral meningitis after enteroviruses. Herpes viruses enter the meninges and CSF by traveling along nerves that lead into the spine or brain, rather than by entering the bloodstream.

Flaviviruses are the viruses carried by mosquitoes that can cause meningitis or encephalitis (an infection and inflammation of the brain). West Nile virus has become an important cause of viral meningitis since it first entered the United States in 1999. Another flavivirus that can cause meningitis is the virus that causes St. Louis encephalitis.

Other viruses that may cause viral meningitis include HIV, cytomegalovirus (a kind of herpes virus), adenoviruses (one cause of the common cold), influenza viruses, and rarely, the viruses that cause mumps and measles (among unvaccinated children).

OTHER TYPES OF MENINGITIS

Fungi (the plural of fungus) cause many human diseases, including the common skin conditions athlete's foot and ringworm (yes, it's a fungus, not a worm). One fungus known as *Cryptococcus neoformans* can cause a dangerous form of meningitis. Cryptococcus (often called crypto for short) is found worldwide in soil and in bird droppings. (So stay away from that pigeon-poop-covered statue in the park!) Crypto can float in the air, and people inhale tiny bits of the fungus. Once inside the lungs, the fungus can travel through the bloodstream to the meninges and brain.

Most healthy people won't get sick if they are exposed to crypto. But crypto is very dangerous for people with weakened immune systems, especially for people infected with HIV. Only about 1 out of every 100,000 healthy people get crypto meningitis. However, between 200 and 700 out of every 100,000 people with AIDS get it. Without treatment, crypto meningitis is usually fatal. With treatment, it still kills more than 1 out of 10 of the people who get it.

Amoebas can also cause meningitis. Amoebas are the most primitive animals. Even though amoebas are larger than bacteria, you still need a microscope to see these tiny parasites (harmful organisms that live in or on another organism). The amoeba called *Naegleria fowleri* causes an especially deadly kind of meningitis that infects the brain as well as the meninges. The amoeba is found around the world in bodies of warm freshwater, such as ponds, lakes, and hot springs. The amoeba can even be found in swimming pools that have not been properly treated with chlorine.

People pick up *Naegleria* when they swim or dive in contaminated waters. The amoebas penetrate the mucous membranes of the nose and sinuses and travel along the nerves to infect the spinal cord and brain. Meningitis caused by this nasty amoeba is rare—which is fortunate, because it kills 95 out of every 100 people that it infects.

Because meningitis caused by fungi and amoebas is so unusual, the following chapters will focus on meningitis caused by bacteria and viruses. Read on to see how people can develop different kinds of bacterial and viral meningitis depending on their age.

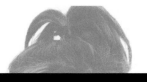

Chapter 3

MENINGITIS THROUGH THE LIFESPAN

Elise's Story

Elise was sick even before she was born. Monitors strapped to her mother's belly showed Elise's heart beat was slowing to a dangerously low rate. When Elise's mom developed a fever during the long labor, the doctor suspected both Elise and her mother had an infection of some kind.

When Elise was finally born, she also had a fever. There were other signs that something was wrong. Newborns have soft spots on the tops of their heads called fontanels. Normally the fontanels are flat, but Elise's was bulging outward. And her arms and legs were as floppy as a rag doll's. Elise's cry sounded like a mewling kitten instead of the usual lusty cry of a newborn. Nurses rushed the baby off to a neonatal intensive care

People tend to develop different kinds of meningitis at different times in their life. A newborn is less likely to get the type of meningitis that a high school senior would get. And an older adult is probably not going to get the same kind of meningitis that a ten-year-old would get. Because so many organisms can cause meningitis (bacteria, viruses, fungi, and parasites), people may become infected with differing organisms in various ways during their lifetime. Having meningitis once does not protect you against getting another kind of meningitis in the future.

Two factors account for the variety of meningitis infections in differing age groups. The first factor is exposure—that is, which organisms does the person come into contact with? For example, only newborns are exposed to one particular type of bacterium because it is often found in the mother's birth canal. You can't get meningitis caused by the West Nile virus unless a mosquito carrying that virus bites you. And you can't get meningitis caused by *Naegleria* without inhaling or swallowing the amoeba while swimming in contaminated water.

The second factor that determines which kind of meningitis someone may come down with is the strength of his or her own immune system. For example, an older adult may be immune to the bacteria that cause meningitis in teens. However, people of any age who have weakened immune systems, such as people infected with HIV, are much more likely to develop meningitis due to the crypto fungus than is a healthy person.

This chapter discusses the various kinds of meningitis that are more likely to develop in certain age groups. Of course, these are not hard and fast rules. Some forms of meningitis can strike anyone at any time, regardless of his or her age. For example, whenever the scalp or skull is injured, bacteria can travel into the brain or meninges, increasing the chance for developing bacterial meningitis. This can happen after head trauma (such as a bad head injury due to an auto accident) or following surgery to the head or brain (such as ear or sinus surgery, or surgery to remove a brain tumor).

NEWBORNS

Newborns are very susceptible to the bacterium *Streptococcus agalactiae* (group B strep, or GBS). About half the cases of newborn bacterial meningitis are caused by GBS. These bacteria live in the gastrointestinal tracts of about one-fourth of all men and women. The bacteria also live in the vagina of about one-fourth of all women. People who carry GBS do *not* have a sexually transmitted disease. GBS bacteria are just one of the many kinds of bacteria that normally live in and on our bodies. While GBS bacteria are not harmful to the people who carry them, they can be deadly for newborns.

Occasionally, babies such as Elise become infected with GBS before birth if the mother's amniotic fluid (the liquid surrounding the baby in the uterus) is infected. This can happen if the bacteria travel upward into the uterus during a long labor, or if the amniotic sac (the protective membranes around the baby) ruptures too soon before birth.

However, most babies become infected with GBS when they swallow or breathe in the bacteria as they move down the birth canal during delivery. GBS infection can cause three common diseases in the newborn: meningitis, septicemia, and pneumonia (an infection of the lungs).

Onset
About half of the babies who become infected with GBS will show signs of illness at birth or within the first week

of life. Doctors call that early-onset infection. The other half develop late-onset illness. These babies become sick when they are between a week and three months old. Many times the source of infection for babies with late-onset GBS infection is not the mother. Perhaps visiting relatives transferred the bacteria from their hands while cuddling the new baby. Doctors can't always figure out how the baby becomes infected.

It can be tricky to tell when a tiny baby is sick with GBS, or any other disease for that matter. An older child might complain of a stiff neck and a headache, but babies can't tell anyone how they're feeling. The signs of illness in a newborn are more subtle. A newborn might have difficulty in nursing or might be irritable and hard to console while crying. The baby could become lethargic (limp, tired, and hard to wake up). A baby with GBS meningitis may have a slight fever, although it will not be as high as the fever that an older child might have. Older children and adults can develop fevers above 104°F (40°C) with meningitis. Any elevation in temperature in a newborn above 99°F (37°C) should be evaluated by a health-care professional.

Really sick babies will have problems breathing. Their heart rates will slow, and their blood pressures will fall. They can have seizures. Their fontanels may bulge due to the swelling and pressure of the meninges and brain. Of the babies who survive GBS meningitis, 1 out of 5 are likely to have severe problems such as cerebral palsy or deafness. Three out of 10 may have milder problems such as learning disorders or long-term behavior problems.

Prevention
While GBS is the most common cause of newborn meningitis in the United States, it is easily prevented. Fifteen years ago, about 7,500 newborns were infected with GBS each year. Currently, fewer than 3,000 babies develop GBS infections annually.

In 1996 the CDC issued new guidelines stating that all pregnant women should be tested for GBS at thirty-five to thirty-seven weeks of pregnancy (a normal pregnancy is forty weeks). If the vaginal secretions from a woman test positive for the bacteria (remember that about one-fourth of all women normally carry GBS), intravenous antibiotics are given to the mother during labor and delivery. This has nearly eliminated the disease among babies of women who receive routine prenatal care.

Less common causes of bacterial meningitis in newborns include *E. coli* (about 30 percent of the cases), and Listeria (5 percent to 20 percent of the cases). Occasionally, newborn meningitis can be caused by other bacteria.

Several kinds of viral meningitis may occur in newborns. The causes include cytomegalovirus and enteroviruses. Herpes simplex, the virus that causes genital herpes, is especially dangerous to newborns. Doctors usually recommend delivery by C-section (cutting open the abdomen and uterus to remove the baby) for mothers with a history of genital herpes. This protects the baby from exposure to the virus during vaginal delivery.

If a woman catches herpes zoster—the virus that causes chickenpox—late in her pregnancy, her baby has a 1 in 4 chance of being infected by the virus during or shortly after delivery. Fortunately, it is rare in the United States for newborns to develop herpes meningitis, because it can be fatal.

Elise spent a total of twelve days in the hospital under close observation. She received intravenous antibiotics to cure her meningitis and made a complete recovery. Elise was lucky—she didn't suffer any permanent complications from her meningitis. These days, she's a happy, healthy young woman getting ready for college. Elise was born before testing of pregnant women for GBS became routine. Since then, cases of GBS meningi-

tis are mostly found among infants of women who were not tested for the bacteria because they did not receive regular prenatal care (for example, recent immigrants or women living in poverty who have no access to medical care).

INFANTS AND CHILDREN

Among all age groups, the risk of meningitis is greatest in children between birth and two years old. After the neonatal period (the first month of life), bacterial meningitis among infants and children is usually caused by one of three types of bacteria: *S. pneumoniae*, *N. meningitidis*, and *H. influenzae*.

S. pneumoniae causes pneumonia, septicemia, and ear and sinus infections, as well as meningitis. This is the most common cause of bacterial meningitis in older infants and children, even though the pneumococcal vaccine can help prevent it. Pneumococcal meningitis occurs most often during the winter months. The bacteria are often passed to children by healthy family members who normally carry pneumococcus in their noses and throats.

Some children are more susceptible than others to infection by this bacterium. For example, children with sickle-cell disease (an inherited disorder that results in abnormal red blood cells and a weakened immune system) are 300 times more likely to come down with pneumococcal meningitis than are children without it. Four out of every 100 children with sickle-cell disease develop pneumococcal meningitis before they turn five years old unless they routinely take antibiotics to help prevent it. It is common for children with sickle-cell disease to receive daily penicillin for the first five or six years of their life. While penicillin doesn't eliminate the bacteria in the nose and throat, it seems to prevent invasive disease (the bacteria entering the blood to cause meningitis and/or septicemia).

N. meningitidis is the second most common (and the most deadly) cause of bacterial meningitis in this age group. If enough of these bacteria enter the bloodstream, children can die within hours. They die so quickly because of the poisonous chemical called endotoxin that these bacteria produce. Most children who get meningo-coccal meningitis are infected at a day care center or by a family member. While this type of meningitis can occur any time of year, it is more common during the winter and spring months.

COCHLEAR IMPLANTS

In 2006 the United States Food and Drug Administration (FDA) issued a warning about an unusual but serious cause of bacterial meningitis in young children. Surgeons have inserted a medical device called a cochlear implant into about 11,000 deaf children. The cochlear implant gives the children the ability to hear some sounds. Most children who receive these implants are under six years old.

Any time doctors insert a foreign object into the body—for example, a pacemaker or a cochlear implant—there's a chance of infection at the surgical site. Doctors followed a group of children with cochlear implants for several years. They discovered the children's risk of contracting pneumococcal meningitis (caused by the bacterium *S. pneumoniae*) was thirty times greater than in children without the implants. The FDA advises parents of children with these implants to watch their children for signs of meningitis, especially fever, headache, stiff neck, nausea, vomiting, irritability, and ear pain.

H. influenzae: The strain of this bacterium known as type B or Hib was once the most common cause of bacterial meningitis in children. Since widespread use of the Hib vaccine for infants and children began in 1987, the disease in young children has fallen by an astonishing 99 percent. Currently, the disease occurs primarily among unvaccinated children. It also strikes those with weakened immune systems who respond poorly to vaccines, such as children with HIV. Hib also causes septicemia and pneumonia

Less common causes of bacterial meningitis in this age group include late-onset GBS, Listeria, Pseudomonas, Campylobacter, Salmonella, Staphylococcus, and the bacteria that cause tuberculosis and Lyme disease.

A major risk factor for bacterial meningitis in babies is the absence of any natural immunity. Breast-fed babies are partially protected for about six months against some of the bacteria that cause meningitis. If the mother has developed immunity to a particular kind of bacterium during her lifetime, her breast milk usually includes antibodies that can protect the nursing infant. However, formula-fed babies and young children can become infected by respiratory secretions of close contacts. A doting grandma whispering into a baby's ear or a four-year-old planting a sloppy wet kiss on his baby sister's cheek can pass on the bacteria.

Onset

The onset of meningitis in infants and children generally occurs in two ways—gradually over days or suddenly over hours. Most often, meningitis is preceded by several days of upper respiratory ailments, such as the sore throat, cough, and stuffy nose that occur with colds and other viral infections such as the flu. The viruses weaken the mucosal linings of the throat and nose, making it easier for resident bacteria to enter the bloodstream. Meningitis symptoms, such as fever, lethargy, and a stiff, painful neck tend to develop gradually over a couple of days.

The early stages of meningitis infection have symptoms similar to the flu or a bad head cold. This makes it hard to diagnose and treat early.

Sometimes meningitis has a sudden, or acute, onset in children, especially when caused by meningococcal bacteria. Infection with this bacterium can cause a child to go from seeming happy and healthy to being near death in twenty-four hours or less. Meningococcal infection results in widespread internal bleeding which damages organs, especially the kidneys and lungs. The poison released by the bacteria significantly weakens the heart. Pressure on the brain caused by infection of the cerebrospinal fluid and meninges may lead to coma and death. Even with prompt and intensive treatment, many children with meningococcal infection die or are left with serious disabilities.

The risk of developing viral meningitis is twenty times higher in infants under one year old than among older children and adults. About 75 percent of all cases of viral meningitis in babies and children under fifteen years old are due to one of the many enteroviruses that live in the intestinal and respiratory tracts. This means that the viruses can be easily passed by younger children who may not have washed their hands thoroughly after going to the bathroom. Or they may be passed by respiratory secretions spread by coughs, sneezes, or contact with saliva or nasal mucus. While viral meningitis can occur at any time of year, it is most common in the summer months.

COMMON SYMPTOMS OF MENINGITIS IN CHILDREN

Infants
- Failure to drink enough fluids
- Vomiting
- Increased irritability
- Increased lethargy
- Fever
- Seizures
- Bulging fontanels

Children one year old and older
- Nausea and vomiting
- Headache
- Increased sensitivity to light
- Fever
- Odd behavior, confusion
- Lethargy
- Seizures
- Stiff or painful neck

TEENS AND YOUNG ADULTS

Infection with meningococcal bacteria is the most common cause of meningitis in teens and young adults. In fact, of all cases of meningococcal meningitis in the United States each year, 3 out of 10 cases occur in this age group. For unknown reasons, this form of meningitis is five times more deadly when it strikes fifteen- to twenty-four-year-olds compared to other age groups. Meningococcal meningitis kills nearly 25 percent of adolescents and young adults who get it, compared to about 10 percent of the general population.

Meningococcal bacteria are more likely to colonize a young person than an older one. About 1 in 10 people in the general population are colonized with *N. meningitidis*. But among young adults, about 1 in 4 is colonized with the bacteria. In addition, many activities that young adults commonly engage in, such as not eating well and not sleeping enough, are known to weaken the immune system. A weakened immune system makes it easier to become infected by others. It also makes it easier for a person's own colonized bacteria to break through the protective mucous layers and enter the bloodstream.

After children younger than two years, the single group of people at highest risk for developing meningococcal meningitis is first-year college students living in dorms. According to the CDC, the rate for meningococcal meningitis among first-year college students living in dorms is 5.1 in 100,000 people, compared with 0.6 in 100,000 of all college students. Health experts point out the following factors as contributing to the increased risk for meningococcal meningitis in young people:

- Sharing anything that touches the mouth, such as water bottles, cups, eating utensils, cigarettes
- Sharing personal items, such as toothbrushes or lip balm

- Crowded living conditions, such as in dorms, boarding schools, and sleep-away camps
- Close contact with respiratory secretions as occurs with kissing, coughing, and sneezing
- Moving to a new residence (increases exposure to new varieties of bacteria perhaps not carried by family and friends)
- Attendance at a new school with students from geographically diverse areas (also increases exposure to new bacteria)
- Drinking alcohol (weakens immune system)
- Active or passive (secondhand) smoking (damages protective linings of nose and throat)
- Irregular sleeping patterns (weakens immune system)

Many colleges educate incoming students about the dangers of meningococcal meningitis and how to avoid it. Some colleges require vaccination prior to admission, while other schools are considering doing so.

Enteroviruses are the most common cause of viral meningitis at every age. Clusters of cases of viral meningitis can occur in schools and colleges during the winter months. While viral meningitis due to herpes viruses is rare, most cases that do occur are found in adolescents and adults. Meningitis due to flaviviruses (such as the one that causes West Nile virus) can occur in this group as well, although it is uncommon.

Meningitis caused by the mumps virus is not common because of widespread childhood immunization. However, the cases that do occur tend to peak in males between the ages of sixteen and twenty-one. During the winter of 2005 and into the spring of 2006, hundreds of people in the United States who had previously been vaccinated against mumps came down with the disease. The outbreak suggests that childhood vaccines may lose their effectiveness over time. They may not offer permanent protection against meningitis caused by the mumps virus.

ADULTS

Bacterial meningitis in adults may follow surgery. Or it can occur after other bacterial infections such as ear or sinus infections, pneumonia, endocarditis (an infection of the heart valves), and osteomyelitis (an infection of a bone). Other risk factors for bacterial meningitis in adults include age (being older than sixty-five), diabetes, alcoholism, and intravenous drug use. Some medical treatments may also put people at risk. Chemotherapy treatment for cancer, immunosuppressant treatment for organ transplant patients (given so the patients' immune systems don't reject the transplanted organs), and the presence of implanted medical devices (such as pacemakers) may leave patients vulnerable to bacterial meningitis.

Among adults, 8 out of 10 cases of bacterial meningitis are caused by *S. pneumoniae* and *N. meningitidis*. In adults, meningitis caused by *S. pneumoniae* is the more serious disease, because many adults will have developed at least a partial immunity to some strains of meningococcus. Between 19 percent and 37 percent of adults who develop pneumococcal meningitis die even with treatment, and nearly a third are left with serious disabilities such as deafness or mental impairment. Only 3 percent to 13 percent of adults who develop meningococcal meningitis die, a much smaller number than in children, teens, and young adults.

In adults over the age of fifty, Listeria is a common cause of bacterial meningitis too. *H. influenzae* meningitis used to be more common in adults. However, the widespread vaccination of infants with the Hib vaccine has helped to protect adults as well. A less common cause of bacterial meningitis in adults is due to *S. aureus* (staph). While accounting for only 1 percent to 3 percent of cases, *S. aureus* meningitis kills about half of adults who contract it. Increasingly, many staph infections are resistant to the antibiotics that once promptly cured them.

About 75 percent of adults who come down with meningitis become ill gradually over one to seven days. The remainder become suddenly ill over twenty-four hours or so. Those who become suddenly sick are often infected by meningococcal meningitis. Read on to discover why meningococcal infections are so deadly, especially for young people.

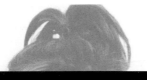

Chapter 4

MENINGOCOCCAL MENINGITIS AND SEPTICEMIA

Andy's Story

Andy Marso was on top of the world. The twenty-two-year-old senior was due to graduate from the University of Kansas School of Journalism in a few weeks. He'd already been offered his dream job as a sportswriter. And Andy and two friends had just signed a lease on an apartment they would share after graduation. But on a Tuesday night, Andy suddenly became sick with chills, fever, and weakness. He retreated to his dorm room and went to bed. It's just the flu, he told himself. Then, at five o'clock on Wednesday morning, Andy climbed out of bed to get a drink of water. He was shaking with chills and fever, and his feet hurt so much he could hardly walk to the bathroom.

Andy returned to bed thinking he'd sleep it off. A friend checked in later that same morning. He saw purple, blotchy bruises covering Andy's arms. He wasn't sure what it meant, but he knew that it didn't look like the flu! Two friends carried Andy to the college health clinic, even though he kept saying that he didn't want to go. Those friends saved Andy's life. As soon as the clinic doctor saw Andy, she arranged for an air ambulance transfer to the University of Kansas Medical Center.

In just hours, people infected with meningococcal bacteria can go from seeming perfectly healthy to being critically ill. A college student such as Andy can attend class in the morning and by nightfall be in an ICU, hooked up to a ventilator and getting medications to support his failing kidneys and heart. A cranky toddler with a fever can go down for a nap and wake up with the purple rash of meningococcal disease over her legs, predicting the possible amputation of toes or feet.

Meningococcal infection is such an alarming disease that local newspapers and television stations usually carry stories about anyone in the community who comes down with it. Fortunately, meningococcal disease is as not common in the United States as it may seem. According to the CDC, between 2,000 and 3,000 Americans become infected with meningococcus each year. Between 9 percent and 12 percent of those people die, even with the best medical care. And up to 20 percent of survivors are left with serious neurological problems, such as deafness, seizures, or brain damage.

Even more deadly is meningococcal septicemia, in which the bacteria in the blood overwhelm the body's natural defenses. Septicemia causes shock (a condition in which blood pressure falls dangerously low), hemorrhage, and damage to internal organs. Many survivors are left with weakened hearts or kidneys. Often, fingers and toes, hands and feet, or even arms and legs are so badly damaged that they must be removed. Because meningococcal meningitis and meningococcal septicemia so often occur together, it is important to know about both of them.

GETTING SICK

Humans are the only host for meningococcal bacteria. The bacteria live in the human nasopharynx—the place where the back of the nasal passages open into the back of the throat. Overall, between 5 percent and 10 percent of people (and up to 25 percent of young adults) are colonized with the bacteria. They naturally harbor the bacteria in their nasopharynx. These people aren't sick. They are asymptomatic carriers, meaning they are healthy and have no symptoms, even though the bacteria are living in them. Most people develop a natural immunity to the bacteria by the time they are thirty years old because of colonization or repeated exposure to the bacteria. That's why meningococcal infection is much more common among children and teens.

People who don't develop immunity are at risk of infection. We don't get infected with meningococcal bacteria by eating contaminated food or by being bitten by an infected mosquito. We don't even get infected by being in the same room with a sick person or by breathing the same air. We *do* become infected by being in very close contact with someone who naturally harbors meningococcal bacteria or by being in close contact with someone who is sick with it.

Close contact means breathing in the tiny airborne respiratory secretions that are spewed out during a cough or a sneeze. However, meningococcal bacteria are most easily spread by direct contact with infected saliva. This includes sharing drinks, food, and eating utensils, taking a drag on someone else's cigarette, and kissing. In fact, a 2006 medical study found that kissing multiple partners quadrupled a teen's risk of developing meningococcal meningitis.

The moist mucous membranes that line our mouth, throat, and nose serve as barriers to help protect us against invading organisms. But the mucous membranes can be damaged or weakened by smoking or by infections such as strep throat, a cold, or the flu. Anything that damages the mucous membranes makes it easier for the meningococcal bacteria to enter the body. So it's not surprising that meningococcal infections often follow viral infections. Yet many cases of meningococcal meningitis are not preceded by infections of any kind. People with weakened immune systems are more likely to get meningitis. Doctors don't yet know all the reasons why one person gets infected while another does not.

Invisible Invaders

It's important to understand the concept of invasive disease when talking about meningococcal infection. Imagine a movie theater inside a huge complex—one of those places where a gazillion movies are playing at the same time. There's a big lobby and half a dozen hallways leading off to each theater. A set of sturdy wooden doors separates each theater from its hallway. Think of the hallways as your throat, and the doors leading into each theater as the protective cells that line your throat. The theater itself, where you sit watching the latest action thriller with your friends, represents the blood vessels that run behind the cells lining your throat.

Imagine that some jerks are messing around outside the movie complex. Oddly enough, the words N. *meningitidis* are printed on the backs of their filthy shirts. They're trying to get inside without paying. Or maybe they want to start a fight with some guys from a rival school who are already inside. The bad guys are skulking around the ticket booths, and some manage to get into the lobby. But that's okay; they really can't do much harm there. They're just hanging out, colonizing the place.

Then the bad guys spread out into the hallways leading to each theater, looking for trouble. The real danger occurs when the bad guys kick down the doors and barge into the theater where you're watching the movie. Maybe the doors weren't as sturdy as they were supposed to be. Maybe termites have weakened the doors—just as a recent infection might weaken the layer of protective cells in our bodies. In any event, the doors can no longer keep the bad guys out of the theater. They just shove their way inside. Remember that in our scenario, the theater is your bloodstream. Now you're infected.

In some cases, ushers actually escort the bad guys through the doors and into your theater! Our bodies may be tricked into "thinking" the meningococcal bacteria are food. The bacteria glom onto the cells with their pili—those tiny hairlike projections that allow them to grasp cell walls. The cell may enclose the bacteria in hollow spaces called vesicles (sort of like a clear plastic hamster ball). Then the cell transports the bacteria, safely hidden inside the vesicles, across the cell. Next, the cells carry the bacteria into our bloodstreams (or, in the case of our scenario, into our theater) as if they were bits of tasty food destined to nurture our bodies.

Now these bad guys—the colonizing meningococcal bacteria—are no longer harmless. They have become invaders. Once the bacteria penetrate the protective cells lining our throats and enter our bloodstreams, they become what's called invasive meningococcal disease. These bacteria double in number every thirty minutes. It doesn't take long before their numbers are overwhelming.

Having invasive meningococcal disease means that the bacteria are in the blood. That's how it starts. But these nasty bugs are not very picky. Once the bacteria are cruising in the bloodstream, they readily find new homes in the lungs and other hidden corners of the body. About half of the time, the bacteria pass from the blood into the CSF and the meninges to cause meningitis. About one-third of the time, the massive numbers of bacteria overwhelm the body's immune system, and septicemia results.

Meningococcal septicemia is life-threatening. It kills 4 out of 10 people who develop it. That's a lot higher than the average 1 out of 10 people who die from meningococcal meningitis. Septicemia can happen with or without having meningitis, although they often occur in the same patient, as we'll see with Andy Marso. When invasive meningococcal disease occurs without meningitis, it may cause infections in the lungs, joints, inner ears, and urinary tract.

> *At the University of Kansas Medical Center, doctors were pretty sure that Andy had meningococcal meningitis and septicemia. Shortly after noon on Wednesday, a staff member called Andy's parents in Minnesota to let them know that their son was very sick. Andy had phoned his mom just the night before, telling her that he had the flu. Now doctors said he was in critical condition! Andy's mom and dad got on the next flight to Kansas. At the hospital, Andy's parents were shocked to see that his breathing was labored and his heart was beating nearly 150 times a minute. His fever had soared to 104°F (40°C). Minutes later, a nurse took Andy's parents to a waiting room while doctors put a tube down Andy's throat so that he could be hooked up to a ventilator.*

MENINGOCOCCAL MENINGITIS

Meningococcal bacteria reproduce rapidly when they first enter the CSF because the CSF has very few white blood cells to fight off the initial invasion. But some white blood cells do eventually reach the CSF and the meninges, ready to do their job. There are several kinds of white blood cells. Some act as the predatory hunter-killers of our immune systems. They literally gobble up many of the bacteria and dissolve them. Other white blood cells release chemicals that help kill more bacteria.

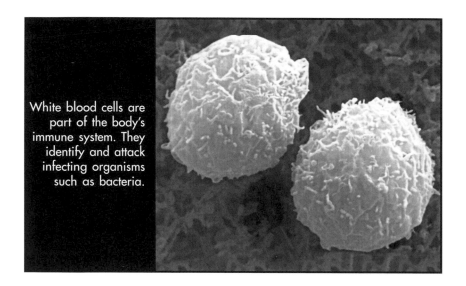

White blood cells are part of the body's immune system. They identify and attack infecting organisms such as bacteria.

Once each white blood cell completes its task, it dies. More white blood cells move into the CSF as replacements for the ones that die.

White blood cells are part of the body's inflammatory response, one way in which your immune system fights off infections. Think of a time when you might have had an infected cut on your finger. The inflammatory response is what caused the redness, swelling, heat, and pus (largely made up of dead white blood cells and destroyed bacteria) in your finger. Your body cured the infection, but the cure caused problems of its own, such as that hot, painful throbbing you probably remember having.

Now imagine that the same redness, swelling, heat, and pus are inside your head and along the length of your spinal canal. Much of the damage caused by meningitis is due to the body's natural inflammatory response. The inflammation puts dangerous pressure on the brain. The pressure may cause unusual behavior such as aggression or confusion, seizures, strokes, and coma. The inflammation also causes the fever and headache experienced by meningitis victims. Because the CSF carries the infection down

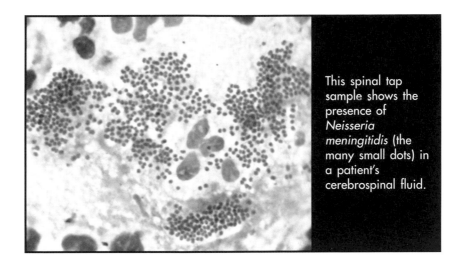

This spinal tap sample shows the presence of *Neisseria meningitidis* (the many small dots) in a patient's cerebrospinal fluid.

the spinal cord, people often have severe pain and stiffness in their necks and backs.

Inflammation is not the only thing that causes increased pressure in the brain. Specialized cells deep inside the brain continuously produce about 1 to 2 teaspoons (7 to 10 milliliters) of CSF. After CSF circulates throughout the spinal canal and the meninges, another area in the brain absorbs it. A new batch begins circulating. In a healthy person, the amount of CSF circulating is constant.

Pus can block the canals where the CSF circulates within the brain. If CSF cannot circulate properly, it cannot be reabsorbed. The brain keeps on producing CSF, but there's no place for it to go. It's a bit like a leaky faucet dripping into a sink. As long as the drain is open, the sink will not run over. But if you put a stopper in the drain, eventually, the sink will fill up and overflow.

The CSF, however, cannot overflow like a sink. Instead, it keeps building up, leading to an extreme amount of pressure on the brain and the meninges. As pressure inside the brain rises, vital areas of the brain that

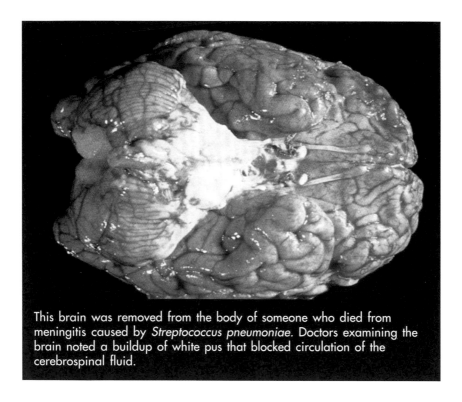

This brain was removed from the body of someone who died from meningitis caused by *Streptococcus pneumoniae*. Doctors examining the brain noted a buildup of white pus that blocked circulation of the cerebrospinal fluid.

control breathing, blood pressure, and heart rate are damaged. People can die of these complications of meningitis even if they do not develop septicemia.

When doctors suspect invasive meningococcal disease, they quickly give large doses of antibiotics, most often a form of penicillin. Fortunately, meningococcal bacteria are seldom resistant to penicillin, unlike some other bacteria that have become resistant to penicillin and other antibiotics.

MENINGOCOCCAL SEPTICEMIA

As bad as meningococcal meningitis is, meningococcal septicemia is worse. Remember, septicemia can occur with or without meningitis. Some people with invasive meningococcal disease only have meningitis. Some only have septicemia. But many victims of meningococcal disease have both meningitis and septicemia, just like Andy did. Both must be considered in order to understand the devastating effects of invasive meningococcal infection.

One of the most dangerous problems with meningococcal disease is the poison that the bacteria produce. Meningococcal bacteria are surrounded by a slimy cell wall that contains endotoxin. Many bacteria produce endotoxin, but meningococcal bacteria churn out one hundred to one thousand times more endotoxin than most other kinds of bacteria produce.

As meningococcal bacteria multiply and move through the bloodstream, they shed bubbles of concentrated endotoxin. The circulating bubbles seem to act like decoys, making it hard for the immune system—the white blood cells and antibodies—to distinguish the bacteria from the bubbles. The antibiotics start killing off the bacteria right away. But as antibiotics kill the meningococcal bacteria, they release even more endotoxin as they disintegrate. For a while, the increase in circulating endotoxin makes the patient get even worse.

Eventually, antibiotics and a strong immune system may be able to successfully destroy the bacteria. However, antibiotics have no effect on the endotoxin bubbles. The bubbles are not living organisms like bacteria. They're like tiny balloons filled with poison instead of air. The bubbles continue to release endotoxin into the bloodstream until they finally empty out and deflate.

Endotoxin Damage

Meningococcal septicemia is very dangerous for two reasons. First, the endotoxin seems to specially target the heart. When the endotoxin reaches the heart, it partially paralyzes the heart muscle, affecting its ability to pump efficiently. To see how this works, make a tight fist. Clench it over and over again. Squeeze. Relax. Squeeze. Relax.

That is how a normal heart pumps. Then make a loose fist. Instead of clenching your hand, barely twitch your fingers. That's how a heart damaged by endotoxin beats. Instead of a strong, vigorous *lub-DUB, lub-DUB*, the heart makes a feeble *lub-lub, lub-lub*. It's as if a once-strong muscle has gone flabby. Blood pressure may fall dangerously low. Organs suffer from lack of oxygen. Powerful medications are required to support the failing heart.

The second reason meningococcal septicemia is so dangerous is the damage the endotoxin does to blood vessel walls. White blood cells are abundant in the bloodstream. They readily lock onto and engulf meningococcal bacteria. When the white blood cells come into contact with the bacteria's endotoxin, the cells release chemicals that make the inside linings of blood vessels sticky. The white blood cells then get trapped on the sticky blood vessel walls. The lining of the damaged blood vessel walls gradually peels off and is stripped away.

Blood cells called platelets rush in to plug up the ruined vessel walls. The platelets help to form blood clots, which normally would be useful in repairing the damage. However, the endotoxin also damages proteins that control the body's blood-clotting process. Within minutes, the platelets go wild, forming millions of tiny clots in blood vessels all over the body, even in undamaged blood vessels. The clots further damage the injured blood vessel walls. The blood vessels disintegrate, allowing blood to leak into surrounding tissue. Blood is meant to flow inside arteries, veins, and capillaries. When blood breaks through its confining vessels, it damages and destroys normal tissue.

Often, blood leaks into the kidneys and the lungs, causing serious harm to those important organs. Patients may need to be put on ventilators if the lungs are too damaged. Sometimes the injured kidneys cannot do a good enough job of cleaning the blood. Patients may need to be put on dialysis machines to clean the blood until the kidneys can recover.

The distinctive purple rash of meningococcal septicemia is caused by blood leaking from the broken blood vessels under the skin. The rash starts out looking like tiny purple or red-purple dots. The rash may be found on a patient's abdomen or back, on arms and fingers, and often on the feet and hands. As the bleeding continues, the dots get bigger and join together to form areas that look like huge, mushy bruises. The skin and underlying muscles are destroyed.

The damage can be so severe that the skin cells or muscles can't regenerate or repair themselves. This is why people with meningococcal septicemia may lose their fingers and toes. Sometimes hands, feet, or even entire limbs must be amputated to save the patient's life. The rash occurs in about 9 out of 10 young people who come down with meningococcal disease. It occurs less often in older people.

People with invasive meningococcal disease are critically ill. Doctors will usually put these patients in an ICU. The patients will be hooked up to machines that monitor their heartbeat, their blood pressure, and perhaps their brain waves. They may receive a dozen intravenous medications. Even with antibiotics and the very best medical care, it can take two or more days for the endotoxin to clear the body. In the meantime, the endotoxin continues to circulate in the blood, damaging organs and destroying blood vessels.

At first, Andy's parents didn't think he would even make it through the night. His organs started to fail. His fingers and toes turned black. But he did live, largely due to the machines and medications helping him out. It took two weeks to clear the endotoxins from Andy's body. Even as Andy recovered from the infection, his fingers and toes continued to get worse. The blackened dead skin seemed to march upward from his fingers and toes to his hands and feet. His first amputation surgery—to remove his lifeless toes—was scheduled.

It may take days or even weeks for someone to recover from a meningococcal infection. Some lucky people have a complete recovery, while many others face permanent physical disabilities or mental impairment. Family and friends will likely have to offer support and help for a long period of time. Will the patient need follow-up medical care or physical therapy to regain her strength? Will she need counseling so she can learn to live with her new limitations?

Schools and workplaces may need to make adaptations so that the patient can return to as normal a life as possible. Will the person recovering from meningococcal disease need a lighter class load or special tutoring so that he can catch up with other students? If he can return to work, will he need a reduced work schedule? Will he suffer from aggression, mood swings, or depression?

Despite the terrible toll invasive meningococcal disease takes on its victims, it remains a relatively rare disease in the United States. In other parts of the world—for example, in Africa's meningitis belt—many parents live in daily fear of discovering the deadly meningococcal rash on their children's bodies. And health-care workers in those areas must all too often face the fact that there is little they can do to save those children once meningococcal disease strikes.

Andy's doctors said he suffered an unusually large amount of skin damage with his meningococcal infection. Nearly one-third of his skin was affected, leaving him looking like he'd been burned in a fire. Andy spent a total of 141 days in the hospital. During ten different surgeries, doctors performed skin grafts (attaching fresh skin to damaged areas) to save what areas they could. Even with the best medical care, Andy lost all his toes, and his feet were amputated nearly to the arch. On his hands, all his fingers were amputated, leaving only one thumb.

Andy still faces years of therapy and rehabilitation to learn to use the new prosthetic devices attached to what remain of his hands and feet. In spite of everything, Andy still looks forward to a career in journalism when his recovery is complete. Andy's good friend Clay Britton said, "Andy doesn't feel sorry for himself, although he has every right to. I don't think anyone doubts Andy will be able to do whatever he wants in life."

Later, doctors learned that the particular strain of meningococcal bacteria that had sickened Andy could not have been prevented by any vaccine available in the United States. However, as shown in the next chapter, vaccines can help to prevent other strains of meningococcal meningitis, as well as meningitis caused by pneumococcus and Hib.

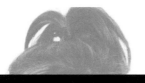

Chapter 5

PREVENTION OF MENINGITIS

Stopping an Outbreak

In 2006 nine students at the University of Louisiana in Lafayette were stricken with meningococcal meningitis. Three of them died while the other six recovered. The university decided to vaccinate an estimated 6,500 students against the disease. Nearly 4,000 students were vaccinated the first weekend alone. While the vaccine normally costs $105 a dose, the Louisiana State Health Department footed the bill in an attempt to stop the spread of the deadly disease.

Vaccinations started with a small group of people closely associated with the victims. The vaccination campaign then expanded in stages to include all campus residents and students twenty years old

*and younger. "This is really a preventive measure,"
said state epidemiologist Dr. Raoult Ratard. "It's
always a good idea to get a vaccination."*

In 1796 English doctor Edward Jenner vaccinated eight-year-old James Phipps against a serious disease called smallpox. Since then, doctors have looked for better ways to prevent diseases, not just treat them. The next vaccine was used in 1885, when Louis Pasteur successfully vaccinated a boy named Joseph Meister for rabies after Joseph was bitten by a rabid dog. By the early 1900s, vaccination had become a familiar word to many people even though scientists were not sure how vaccines worked. It took a long time to even begin to understand how the human immune system operates. We're still learning.

Our immune system is a wonderfully complicated process for protecting our bodies against invading organisms such as bacteria and viruses. Let's say you accidentally slash your foot on a rusty nail. A gang of dangerous bacteria enters your body through the cut. The bacteria carry antigens on the surface of their cells. Antigens are like little photo I.D. tags that reveal the true identity of the invaders. In this case, let's imagine that the tough guys are tetanus bacteria.

Should you be worried? Surprise! Your body knows all about tetanus. When you were a little kid you were vaccinated against tetanus, a potentially deadly disease. The tetanus vaccine stimulated your body to form tetanus antibodies. Antibodies are protein molecules arranged in a Y-shape that attack and destroy a specific organism (such as the tetanus bacteria). Antibodies fit into the antigen like a key fits into a lock. Only one antibody can attach to the antigen of a specific kind of microorganism and kill it.

In some cases, once you've caught a disease—for example, measles—the formation of antibodies against measles protects you from ever getting sick with it again. But, luckily, you don't have to get sick with a disease to be protected against it. That's what vaccines do for you. When a doctor gives a little boy his DTaP shot (for diphtheria, tetanus, and acellular pertussis or whooping cough), the child's body forms antibodies against all three diseases. It's as if the boy had caught all three of the diseases at the same time and recovered from them. He has all the antibodies he needs to fight off diphtheria, tetanus, and whooping cough, and he's unlikely to catch any of those diseases in the future.

Yet vaccines don't work well against all diseases. For example, scientists have not yet been able to make a dependable vaccine against strep throat, the common cold, or HIV. And in many cases, people need routine booster shots (repeated vaccinations given at specified periods) to maintain their immunity to a particular disease. For example, doctors recommend that people have a tetanus booster every ten years.

Scientists are also finding out that some childhood vaccinations don't necessarily last forever. In 2006, hundreds of fully vaccinated people in the Midwest came down with mumps, putting them at risk for meningitis caused by the mumps virus. Then there are the flu viruses. They mutate so quickly that scientists must develop a new vaccine each year to fight the strain of flu virus that is expected to circulate that year.

Vaccines to protect against bacterial meningitis were among the last of all vaccines to be developed. While many vaccines have been available for decades, the first meningitis vaccine didn't come out until the 1980s. Still, development of vaccinations against bacterial meningitis has been one of the big successes of recent medical history. Millions of young lives have been saved by vaccinations against Hib, meningococcus, and pneumococcus, the three bacteria responsible for most cases of meningitis.

VACCINE SIDE EFFECTS

None of the meningitis vaccines can cause disease, but some people may experience minor side effects. These include swelling, redness, warmth, and pain at the injection site. Side effects can be treated for the first forty-eight hours with cool compresses applied for ten minutes every few hours. If the swelling persists after that time, contact your nurse or doctor.

Some people may develop a mild fever, a headache, or achy muscles after a vaccination. In babies under six months old, these can be treated with the fever-reducing medication acetaminophen (brand name Tylenol). With a doctor's permission, older babies may take either ibuprofen (brand names Advil and Motrin) or acetaminophen. Children and adolescents may take ibuprofen or acetaminophen unless their doctors have told them otherwise (for example, ibuprofen may not be recommended for some people with asthma because they can be allergic to it).

People under eighteen years old should *never* take aspirin or any product containing aspirin without the specific approval of a doctor because of the possibility of a rare but deadly condition called Reye's syndrome associated with its use.

HIB VACCINES

The *H. influenzae* bacterium can cause meningitis, pneumonia, septicemia, infections of the bones, joints, and skin, and a dangerous inflammation of the epiglottis (the piece of cartilage that moves to cover the airway while swallowing). Until a vaccine was developed, *H. influenzae* was deadly for young victims. For example, one study in the 1920s tracked children at Boston Children's Hospital who had meningitis caused by *H. influenzae*. The study found that 77 of the 78 children died of the disease, nearly a 99 percent death rate.

H. influenzae has six strains: A, B, C, D, E, and F. Type B (Hib) causes 95 percent of invasive disease (meningitis, septicemia, and pneumonia). Young children are by far the most susceptible to this infection. The first vaccine for Hib was developed in the United States in 1985. However, it had limited effectiveness at preventing disease. A more effective vaccine became available in 1987.

Prior to the introduction of the Hib vaccine, as many as 20,000 children under five years old in the United States (or about 1 out of every 200) became infected by *H. influenzae* each year. In just fifteen years, the incidence of this type of meningitis fell by an astounding 99 percent. Currently, fewer than 75 cases of Hib infection occur in the United States each year, and most of those are among unvaccinated children or those who did not receive the entire course of recommended vaccinations.

Three vaccine formulations are used in the United States—the PedvaxHib, Comvax, and the DTaP/Hib combination (includes vaccines for diphtheria, tetanus, whooping cough, and Hib). According to the CDC immunization schedule, infants who receive either of the first two vaccines should be vaccinated at two and four months old, with a third injection given between twelve and fifteen months of age. The DTaP/Hib vaccine may be used for the third injection if the doctor prefers.

Infant injections are generally given into the thigh muscle because the hip muscles of children who don't yet walk are too underdeveloped for injections. Common reactions after any immunization can include warmth, redness, swelling, and pain at the injection site. Some children will develop a slight fever, although about 1 out of 20 children will have a fever over 101°F. These are all normal reactions.

MENINGOCOCCAL VACCINES

N. *meningitidis* can cause meningitis, septicemia, pneumonia, arthritis, and urinary tract infections. Humans are the only natural host for this bacterium, which live primarily in the respiratory tract. During the early part of the twentieth century, 8 out of 10 people with meningococcal meningitis died. Outbreaks of meningitis in U.S. Army boot camps during the late 1960s helped spur research on a vaccine against meningococcal disease. While it is relatively uncommon, N. *meningitidis* is the deadliest cause of meningitis in children and young adults.

There are twelve serotypes of N. *meningitidis*, and vaccines work against only some of them. A serotype is the difference in the sugary molecules that make up the capsule that surrounds the bacterium. Imagine a pair of identical twin sisters, one dressed in blue jeans and a red shirt and the other in a green dress. The twins have exactly the same genetic makeup; only their clothing is different. N. *meningitidis* bacteria are like that. Under their capsules (clothing), the bacteria are the same. The structure of the capsules is what distinguishes the serotypes. But those minor differences in the capsules are enough to make some of the serotypes more dangerous than others.

The twelve serotypes of meningococcal bacteria are known as A, B, C, H, I, K, L, W-135, X, Y, Z, and 29E. However, just five serotypes—A, B, C, Y, and W-135—are responsible for 95 percent of meningococcal infections around the world. In the United States, B, C, and Y cause most cases of meningococcal meningitis, although serotypes A and W-135 do occasionally occur. Even though type B is to blame for nearly a quarter of cases of meningococcal disease, no vaccine for it is yet available in the United States.

Two vaccines to help prevent meningococcal disease are licensed for use in the United States. They are Menomune and Menactra.

Menomune is also known as the meningococcal tetravalent polysaccharide vaccine (MPSV4). This vaccine has been around since 1981 and offers protection for types A, C, Y, and W-135, which account for about 7 out of 10 cases of meningococcal disease in the United States. The immunity it offers lasts three to five years. It is safe to use in children between the ages of two and ten years old, although it is generally given only to children with weakened immune systems. The Menomune injection is given under the skin with a short needle.

Menactra is also known as the meningococcal conjugate vaccine (MCV4). This vaccine has been in use since 2005, and it offers protection for the same four serotypes as Menomune. Menactra is approved for ages eleven to fifty-five years old, meaning that more people can benefit from this vaccine. Menactra may offer a stronger and longer-lasting immunity than Menomune, but doctors are not yet sure how long the immunity will last since the vaccine is so new.

The vaccine also helps to reduce colonization with *N. meningitidis*. This helps protect even people who are not vaccinated from infection. Menactra is usually injected into the large deltoid muscle of the upper arm.

The CDC recommends this vaccine be given to all children when they are eleven or twelve years old. Adolescents who were not vaccinated at that age should receive a dose at age fifteen or when they enter high school. All first-year college students who will be living

Arnold Steigerwalt, a CDC research chemist, analyzes samples at the Meningitis and Special Pathogens branch of the National Center for Infectious Diseases. The center studies meningitis in hopes of finding more effective vaccines and treatments for the disease.

in dorms should consider receiving the vaccine if they have never had it. The CDC's goal is for Menactra to be given routinely to every child between the ages of eleven and twelve by 2008. So many children were vaccinated with Menactra in 2006 that the vaccine was in short supply for a few months.

In April 2006, the CDC reported that eight people between the ages of seventeen and nineteen who had received Menactra had developed a rare but serious condition called Guillain-Barré syndrome about six weeks after vaccination. Guillain-Barré is a paralysis of the muscles that starts from the legs and moves upward. At its worst, Guillain-Barré can paralyze the diaphragm so people need a ventilator to help them breathe.

Most people experience a full recovery from the temporary paralysis over several months. It's believed that Guillain-Barré occurs when the immune system is over-stimulated by infections of the respiratory and gastrointestinal tracts, and perhaps also by vaccinations. Often the specific reason why someone develops Guillain-Barré is never known. The condition was most closely linked to people being vaccinated against swine flu in 1976.

While these cases quickly made the news headlines, the CDC pointed out that 1 or 2 people out of 100,000 in this age group normally develop Guillain-Barré each year. The incidence of Guillain-Barré among vaccinated people was in the same range as those who had not been vaccinated. Health officials said there was no evidence that Menactra increased the risk of Guillain-Barré. They urged parents to protect their children with the vaccination.

Jim Garcia, a California man whose son John died of meningococcal disease in 2000 when he was a teenager, is a strong supporter of the vaccine. "Until further tests are done and they can prove a link," Garcia said in an interview, "we may have vaccine out there that can prevent a lot of people from contracting meningococcal meningitis."

Both Menomune and Menactra vaccines are believed to be 85 percent to 100 percent effective at preventing meningococcal infection from the four serotypes included in the vaccines. When a vaccine becomes available for type B, it's likely that health officials will recommend that many people be revaccinated so that they can be protected against that dangerous serotype as well.

Two-thirds of the states have laws that require college students and their parents to be informed about the risk of meningococcal infection before or shortly after starting school. Some colleges are taking it a step further by requiring incoming students who will be living in dorms or residence halls to be vaccinated with Menactra before the school year begins. For example, starting in the fall of 2007, every student moving into campus housing at all colleges

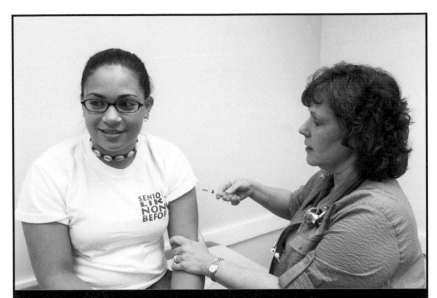

This New Jersey student had to get vaccinated against bacterial meningitis before she could return to school. Many schools, from preschool to college, require such precautionary immunizations.

and universities in Kansas had to be vaccinated against meningococcal meningitis. People who refuse the vaccine must sign a waiver saying that they have been informed of the risks of the disease and that they refuse vaccination in spite of the risks. Additional states are considering such laws for college students.

> *Health-care workers must inform people that the vaccine cannot prevent all strains of meningococcal meningitis. For example, a nineteen-year-old college student named Caitlin Boyle at Marist College on Long Island, New York, died of meningococcal meningitis in 2005, several months after receiving the Menactra vaccine. It's likely that this young woman and Andy Marso, whom we met in the pre-*

vious chapter, had type B meningococcal disease. A vaccine wouldn't have helped either person.

In November 2005, a male first-year student at the University of Michigan developed type C meningococcal meningitis, even though he'd been recently vaccinated. That type is covered in the vaccine. The young man had a full recovery. Health officials say that while it is unfortunate the vaccine didn't prevent him from getting meningitis, it probably decreased the severity of his illness.

PNEUMOCOCCAL VACCINES

S. pneumoniae meningitis was a terrible killer of children before a vaccine became available. In one study of three hundred children in the 1920s who had pneumococcal meningitis, every single child died from it. Pneumococcal disease remains a major source of illness and death in the United States. It causes up to 6,000 cases of meningitis, 50,000 cases of septicemia, 175,000 cases of pneumonia, and perhaps 2 million ear and sinus infections each year.

More than ninety serotypes of pneumococcus exist, and vaccines do not protect against all of the types. Having been infected with one type of pneumococcus or having been vaccinated against it does not protect against the other serotypes. The first vaccine for pneumococcal disease came out in 1977. It was called the pneumococcal polysaccharide vaccine (PPV). However, it only protected against fourteen serotypes. A newer version of PPV (brand name Pneumovax) came out in 1983. PPV offers protection against twenty-three of the serotypes that cause nearly 9 out of 10 pneumococcal infections in the United States. Overall, the PPV prevents 60 percent to 70 percent of invasive pneumococcal disease.

The PPV is recommended for all healthy adults aged sixty-five and older. It is also recommended for certain people in younger age groups who are at high risk for pneumococcal infection (such as people with asthma, diabetes, and heart problems). People who receive their first vaccination before they turn sixty-five will need a one-time booster shot five years later.

The PPV is ineffective at preventing pneumococcal disease in infants and babies, and it is not approved for children under two years old. Fortunately, researchers developed a second vaccine to prevent pneumococcal disease in infants and babies. It's called the pneumococcal conjugate vaccine, or PCV7 (brand name Prevnar), and it came out in 2000. The PCV7 protects against the seven serotypes that cause 8 out of 10 cases of pneumococcal meningitis in children under two years old.

Vaccination against pneumococcal disease has been extremely successful. In one trial, PCV7 reduced invasive pneumococcal disease (which includes meningitis and

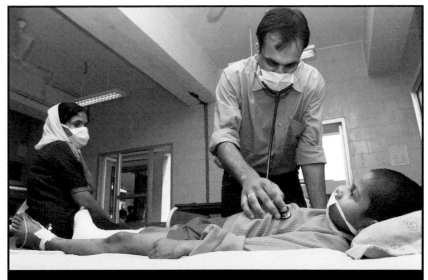

This boy was hospitalized during an outbreak of bacterial meningitis in New Delhi, India, in 2005. The outbreak killed more than 100 people, including many children in poor and crowded neighborhoods.

septicemia) in infants and young children by 97 percent. All children should be vaccinated with PCV7 at two, four, and six months of age. A fourth booster shot should be given between twelve and fifteen months of age.

The widespread use of PCV7 has resulted in two unexpected benefits for society. The first benefit is the decrease in pneumococcal infections in all age groups due to herd immunity. What's herd immunity? It's a theory that the more people who are immune to an infectious disease, the less likely it is that the disease will pass to unprotected people in the same community. Say you've got thirty classmates in your world history class. Twenty-seven of them had a flu shot that year. That greatly reduces the risk of the three people who didn't get a flu shot from catching flu because their herd—the rest of the class—is immune. Experts believe between 80 percent and 95 percent of a population must be vaccinated in order to achieve herd immunity against a given disease.

People vaccinated for pneumococcal infections are less likely to get sick, and therefore, less likely to pass the bacteria on to others. The more people who are vaccinated, the less likely *unvaccinated* people are to come into contact with the bacteria.

Herd immunity is protecting people of all ages against pneumococcal disease. Newborns and very young babies who have not yet been fully vaccinated have 40 percent fewer cases of pneumococcal disease than just a few years ago. While pneumococcal disease was never common in teens and young adults, the rate of infection among this group has fallen to all-time lows. Thank your little brothers and sisters for getting their shots!

The decrease of pneumococcal infections in older adults has been even more dramatic. Since PCV7 was introduced, the incidence of pneumococcal disease in adults over sixty-five years old has dropped by 69 percent. Scientists attribute this remarkable decrease solely to the childhood vaccine. Older adults who have their PPV vaccine reduce their risk for contracting pneumococcal disease even further.

SUMMARY OF MENINGITIS VACCINATIONS

Vaccine	Due at Age:
Hib	2 and 4 months; depending on vaccine used, a third dose may be due at 6 months
Meningococcal	11–12 years old; at 15 if not previously vaccinated; first-year college students living in dorms or group settings; may be recommended for children between 2 and 6 years old with certain medical conditions; also recommended for people traveling to high-risk areas and for adults in high-risk working environments, such as laboratories and military settings.
Pneumococcal	2, 4, and 6 months with a booster shot given between 12 and 15 months; may be recommended for older children with certain medical conditions; also indicated for adults with certain chronic conditions, residents of nursing homes, and everyone 65 years of age or older.

Note: People with chronic health conditions or weakened immune systems should check with their doctors to see if they should receive these vaccinations at different times or more often than recommended.

The other benefit in the widespread use of PCV7 in infants is the reduction of antibiotic-resistant pneumococcal disease. Over the past decade, antibiotics have been used inappropriately in humans and animals. For example, doctors sometimes prescribe antibiotics for people with viral infections even though antibiotics do not kill viruses. Ranchers and farmers feed food laced with antibiotics to their animals and poultry even if the animals are not sick. Healthy animals who receive antibiotics grow faster and bigger than animals who don't receive them.

Because of widespread inappropriate use of antibiotics, bacteria have become increasingly resistant to many antibiotics. Some kinds of bacteria have developed methods for evading death by antibiotic, such as swapping antibiotic-resistant genes with other bacteria and "learning" how to pump antibiotics out of their cells. When someone with a bacterial infection really needs antibiotics, there is a chance the medicine won't work as well as it should.

With fewer pneumococcal infections in every age group, fewer people require treatment with antibiotics. When antibiotics are used less often against specific bacteria, such as pneumococcal bacteria, they are more likely to work when they are really needed. A study published in 2006 showed that penicillin-resistant pneumococcal infections fell 87 percent for the serotypes included in the PCV7 vaccine. This means that when someone develops pneumococcal meningitis, available antibiotics are likely to cure it. That's good news for everyone!

Doctors commonly give preventive antibiotics to people who have been closely exposed to someone with bacterial meningitis. For example, let's say a high school junior who plays basketball is diagnosed with pneumococcal meningitis. Her doctor would recommend that her family and her boyfriend take a course of preventive antibiotics and perhaps get vaccinated as well. The girl's coach might also need antibiotics, as would her teammates and close friends if they had shared water bottles, sodas, lip balms, or eating utensils. Classmates and teachers probably would not need preventive antibiotics unless they had been in very close contact with the girl.

Medical personnel who have cared for someone with bacterial meningitis usually take preventive antibiotics as well, because they are often in very close contact with the patient. This can include the staff in a physician's office and in the ER. If paramedics or emergency medical technicians (EMTs) took the patient to a hospital, they will probably also need preventive antibiotics.

THE BASICS

Old-fashioned common sense can go a long way toward staying healthy. Eat right (especially those fruits and veggies), get enough sleep, and exercise every day (or at least several times a week). Following the four recommendations listed below can help keep infectious diseases such as meningitis, colds, and the flu from tackling you.

Don't share. We all grew up being told sharing is a good thing, and in most cases, it is! But sharing things that touch your mouth can increase the risk of getting meningitis. So when possible, limit the sharing of eating utensils, drinks, water bottles, lip balm, and cigarettes.

Cover up. Cover your mouth and nose with a tissue when coughing or sneezing, and remind your friends to do the same. Use the tissue once, and then throw it away. If you don't have a tissue, cough or sneeze into the crook of your arm. That's better than using your hand. If you cough into your hand, you spread bacteria and viruses to everything you touch for the next hour or so.

Wash your hands. One of the best things you can do to keep from getting sick is to wash your hands thoroughly. Soap interacts with water to loosen dirt, bacteria, and viruses from your skin. Use plenty of soap (it can be plain old soap—antibacterial soaps are not necessary) and warm

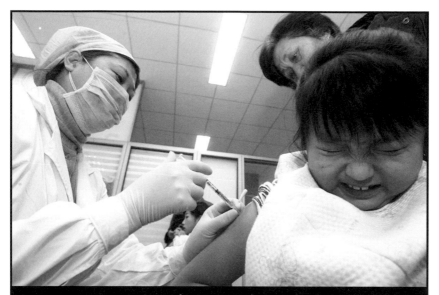

During meningitis outbreaks, the government may require immunizations for young children, who are especially vulnerable to the disease. This girl is getting a vaccination during an outbreak in China.

running water. Wash for twenty seconds. That's about as long as it takes to sing the "Happy Birthday" song twice.

In public restrooms, use a paper towel to turn off the faucet and to open the door when you leave. Alcohol-based hand sanitizers do a good job too. Tuck a few packets of hand wipes into your backpack so that you'll be ready to wash up anywhere. Wash your hands after using the bathroom, before eating, before preparing food, after caring for young children, and after touching surfaces in public places (such as doorknobs, faucets, and shopping carts).

Stay home if you are sick. Too often, people who are sick continue to go to school or work. Maybe there's a big test coming up that you can't miss, or a party you've been looking forward to. Maybe you're worried about missing a day from your weekend job. It's bad for everyone when sick people spread bacteria and viruses around. Staying home keeps you from infecting other people. It also lets you get the rest your body needs while it works to fight off an infection. Instead, keep in touch with your friends by phone, e-mail, or text-message.

Of course, it's still possible for people to come down with meningitis even when they do everything right, such as getting vaccinated and practicing good hygiene. Read the next chapter to learn more about the symptoms of meningitis, and how it is detected and treated.

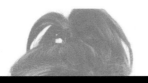

Chapter 6

DIAGNOSIS AND TREATMENT

Joshua's Story

Joshua had stayed home from high school for two days with what seemed to be a stomach virus. On the third day, his nausea and vomiting were gone, so he went back to school. Joshua felt fine all day, but by the next morning, the nausea and vomiting had returned, along with a severe headache, a fever, and body aches. Joshua told his mom he felt rotten. She thought it might be the flu and made an afternoon appointment with the family doctor.

One of the big problems with meningitis is that its early symptoms are much the same as a number of less serious diseases. At first, people may feel general body aches and have a headache. They can develop a fever. People often believe they're coming down with the flu or a cold.

What do most of us do when we feel like we're getting the flu? We go home and rest, maybe drink a glass of juice, and take something for the fever and headache. Maybe a little rash pops up. But people get rashes all the time, don't they?

How can a parent or even a doctor tell the difference between the early onset of meningitis symptoms and those of so many other conditions? The answer is, many times, they can't! For example, a 2006 medical study from the United Kingdom (the UK—England, Scotland, and Wales) shows how difficult diagnosis can be.

In the United Kingdom, meningococcal disease is the most common infectious cause of death among children. It occurs much more often there than it does in the United States, so doctors in the United Kingdom are well aware of the dangers of bacterial meningitis. Even so, the 2006 UK study showed that family doctors sent home *one-half* of the children they saw with early meningococcal disease when their parents first took them into the office for examination. This means that lifesaving treatment is often delayed for several hours. A delay of even a few hours could be the difference between a child living or dying, or between saving or losing fingers and toes.

SYMPTOMS

In the UK study, doctors found that the window of opportunity to diagnose meningococcal disease in children is small. While this particular study looked at children and teens from birth through sixteen years old, its findings apply to other ages as well. Most people who come down with meningococcal disease have only non-specific symptoms, such as a fever or headache, in the first four to six hours of their illness. In many cases, classic meningitis symptoms—rash, stiff neck, and impaired level of consciousness (confusion, lethargy, irritability)—don't develop until thirteen to twenty-two hours from the onset of illness. In the UK study, admission to a hospital occurred, on average, about nineteen hours after the children first started feeling symptoms. By then the children were very sick.

When the UK doctors talked to parents of the 448 children with meningococcal disease they studied, a new pattern of early warning symptoms began to emerge. Parents reported that nearly three-fourths of their children had cold hands and feet, pain in their feet and legs, and an abnormal skin color about eight hours into their illness. Investigators concluded that both doctors and parents relied too much on recognition of later symptoms such as rash, stiff neck, fever, and impaired level of consciousness. Looking for these newly identified symptoms could mean starting vital treatment hours earlier.

Meningitis symptoms can vary greatly. No one person will have all of them, nor will the symptoms always occur in the same order. Symptoms of bacterial meningitis, especially those of meningococcal disease, will develop more suddenly and be more severe. Symptoms of viral meningitis will likely come on more gradually, will be less severe, and are unlikely to produce a rash. Most people with viral meningitis will experience a full and complete recovery.

Nonspecific Symptoms

The incubation period for bacterial meningitis is an average of three to four days, with a range of two to ten days. This means that after people are infected by the bacteria, it will be about three to four days before they start to feel sick. Once people begin to feel sick, things progress very rapidly. The first general symptoms appear within four to six hours after starting to feel sick. These could be symptoms of just about any illness, such as the flu, a cold, or a stomach virus. They largely result from the body's initial response to infection. The following is a list of some of these general symptoms:

- Headache
- Body aches
- Fever
- Nausea and vomiting
- Fatigue
- Loss of appetite

Early Meningitis Symptoms

The next symptoms occur a couple of hours after the non-specific symptoms. They are the newly described symptoms from the UK study. Health officials want everyone to learn to watch out for these symptoms. They result from the beginning of bleeding and circulation problems common with meningococcal infection:

- Cold hands and feet
- Painful feet and legs
- Abnormal skin color (mottling, blue tinge, unusually pale; will vary according to skin color, but the skin will not look normal, regardless of its usual color)

Later Symptoms

These develop an average of thirteen to twenty-two hours after onset of illness. The first three are the so-called "classic" symptoms of meningitis:

Fever. Sometimes people believe they have a fever when their temperature is only slightly elevated. Normal body temperature is 97.6°F (36.4°C) to 99.6°F (37.6°C). People's temperatures can rise one or two degrees when they exercise, when they are in a warm room, or when they are excited or angry. In general, a person's temperature would need to be above 100°F (38°C) while at rest to be considered a fever. With meningitis or septicemia, fevers can soar above 104°F (40°C).

Stiff, painful neck. Because of the inflammation of the meninges, bending the neck or touching the chin to the chest will be very difficult, and it will hurt up and down the length of the spine. A common test that doctors ask people to do is to bring the knee up to the chest while lying down. That movement will be very painful, if not impossible, for someone with meningitis.

Impaired level of consciousness. Because of the increased pressure on the brain, people may become confused, irritable, lethargic, or combative. They will become increasingly difficult to arouse and may later fall into a coma.

Rash. The rash is different from allergic rashes and the spots and bumps of diseases such as measles and chickenpox. Meningococcal rash starts out as small, flat red or purple dots that look like tiny pin pricks. When you press on most rashes, the area briefly turns pale (blanches) or returns to the normal color of the skin. A meningococcal rash does not blanch when pressed. It stays red or purple.

Meningitis support groups recommend the "glass test." Take a clear drinking glass and press the side of it firmly against the skin. You can see through the glass whether or not the rash blanches. If the rash does not blanch, the person needs immediate emergency care at the hospital. Even if it does blanch, it would be best to phone a doctor to ask if a trip to the ER is needed. As time goes on, the small spots get bigger and merge together into huge purple blotchy areas of discolored and dying skin. The same type of rash may appear with both pneumococcal and Hib meningitis as well, but it appears less often and is not as severe.

Extreme sensitivity to light. People with meningitis often complain that even a dim light hurts their eyes and makes their headaches worse.

Seizures. Seizures (a convulsive jerking of the body due to abnormal brain activity) occur in about one-third of meningitis patients.

Complications of Advanced Bacterial Meningitis

Despite the best medical care, some people with meningitis may develop these dangerous and potentially deadly complications:

- Failing heart, lungs, and kidneys
- Massive internal bleeding
- Severe damage to skin, similar to that of a burn victim
- Loss of fingers, toes, hands, feet, and even entire limbs or parts of them
- Deafness, blindness, dizziness, trouble with balance, mental retardation, and learning disabilities.

Leslie Meigs was eight years old when she was diagnosed with a severe case of meningitis. The illness nearly killed her and left her with blotchy scars on her legs.

When Joshua's mom drove him to the doctor's office that afternoon, he slumped in the front seat with his jacket over his head. The light bothered his eyes even though it was a cloudy day. The doctor didn't seem too worried until Joshua complained about how much his neck was hurting. When the doctor asked Joshua to touch his chin to his chest, it hurt too much to do it. Because Joshua had a headache, a fever, a stiff neck, and extreme sensitivity to light, the doctor believed that Joshua had meningitis. The doctor arranged for a specialist to meet Joshua and his mom in the ER of the regional hospital.

DIAGNOSIS

Every minute counts when people have bacterial meningitis, so it's very important for a doctor to figure out what's going on as soon as possible. Bacterial meningitis is not treated in a doctor's office! People who show up at their doctors' offices with possible bacterial meningitis are sent directly to the ER. Many times, parents who worry that their children might have meningitis take them directly to an ER instead of going to their doctors' offices first.

A skilled physician can tell a lot by physical examination of the patient. The ER doctor will look for rash and signs of a stiff neck. She will check that the patient is alert, asking questions to determine the patient's level of consciousness. Does the patient know his name? Does he know where he is and what the date is? The physician will ask family members and friends about the patient's history. Has he been sick for a few days or just a few hours? Has he been around anyone else with similar symptoms—at home, school, church, or sporting activities?

The first and most important test to diagnose meningitis is the spinal tap. In this procedure, a doctor takes a small amount of CSF from the spinal canal for tests. A nurse helps the patient to lie on his side in a fetal position; that is, with neck bent down, knees drawn up, and a curved spine. This position separates the bones of the spine slightly, allowing easier access to the spinal canal.

An area in the lower back is cleansed with an antiseptic solution. The doctor injects a small amount of anesthetic medication such as lidocaine (similar to what the dentist gives you when he fills a cavity in your tooth) to numb the area. Next, the doctor inserts a needle through the skin and into the spinal canal.

She measures the pressure of the CSF with an instrument called a manometer. The normal pressure of CSF is 50 to 180 millimeters of water (written as mm H_2O) in an adult. In a child, it is 30 to 60 mm H_2O. People with meningitis have a very high pressure because of the swelling of the meninges and the surface of the brain. If the disease is advanced, the flow of CSF may be partially blocked by pus, thus further increasing the pressure. CSF pressures commonly reach 200 to 800 mm H_2O or even higher in patients with meningitis.

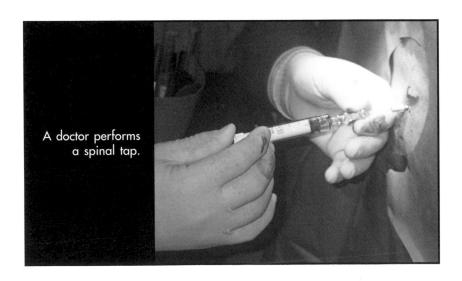

A doctor performs a spinal tap.

89

After the doctor measures the pressure, she allows a small amount of CSF to drip into a tube for testing. Normal CSF is clear. The CSF of someone with bacterial meningitis is cloudy, as if someone had spilled a few drops of milk into it. The CSF is cloudy because of the large numbers of bacteria, protein, and white blood cells in it. High pressure and cloudy fluid indicate that the patient almost certainly has bacterial meningitis. Viral meningitis does not result in cloudy CSF.

The doctor next sends the CSF specimen to the lab where technicians try to identify the organism (bacterium or virus), measure the glucose (sugar) and protein in it, and count the white and red blood cells. The results tell the doctor for sure if bacterial or viral meningitis is present, or if something else such as a stroke or brain tumor might be causing the symptoms.

Additional tests the doctor may perform include:

• Blood tests to look for bacteria and abnormalities such as clotting problems and problems with kidney and liver function
• CT scan of the head to look for inflammation of the meninges and brain
• Chest X-ray to see if the lungs are clear (some meningitis patients will have pneumonia as well)
• EEG (electroencephalogram) to examine the brain waves of people who have or might be having seizures

The first thing the ER doctor did was to give Joshua a huge dose of intravenous penicillin. Next, the doctor performed a spinal tap on Joshua. It didn't hurt as much as Joshua thought it would. Although the pressure of Joshua's cerebrospinal fluid was 475 mm H_2O, the fluid was completely clear. Joshua's mom breathed a sigh of relief when the doctor said it was likely viral meningitis, not bacterial. The doctor sent the CSF and a blood *sample to the lab for examination just to be sure no bacteria were present. By then it was midnight. The doctor kept Joshua in the ER overnight to be sure that he didn't develop a rash or other new symptoms. Joshua dozed on a stretcher behind drawn curtains in a quiet corner of the ER.*

THE HELPFUL HORSE—MENINGITIS ANTISERUM

Antibiotics did not become widely available to treat meningitis and other bacterial infections until the late 1940s. Before then, doctors turned to horses for help! Scientists discovered that if a horse was injected with the blood of a person who had bacterial meningitis, the horse produced antibodies against the bacteria causing the meningitis. Next, scientists drew the horse's blood and extracted the serum. Serum is the clear yellowish fluid left after all the red blood cells, white blood cells, and platelets have been removed. The horse's serum was packed full of beneficial antibodies to fight the meningitis.

The serum containing the meningitis antibodies (called antiserum) could then be given to a person infected with bacterial meningitis. The meningitis antiserum could help a person who was sick with meningitis recover more quickly. It was almost as if the person had developed antibodies on his own. Scientists soon learned how to maintain colonies of bacteria in the laboratory to use in the production of antiserum so that infected human blood was no longer required. However, scientists still needed horses and other animals such as rabbits and sheep to make the antiserum in their blood. They were living, four-footed drug factories.

Meningococcal meningitis: The German physician Dr. G. Jochmann made the first antiserum for meningococcal meningitis in 1906. When antiserum was first used, doctors injected it into patients' veins. American doctor Simon Flexner developed a better method. In 1913 he reported success in curing meningococcal meningitis by injecting the horse antiserum directly into the spinal canal. Used this way, antibodies in the antiserum had direct access to the bacteria circulating in the CSF and could more successfully eliminate them.

The introduction of meningitis antiserum given into the spinal canal dropped the death rate to 2 out of 10 in a 1936 study of 169 children with meningococcal meningitis at Bellevue Hospital in New York. When the first antibiotics for meningococcal disease were introduced a decade later, the death rate for this form of meningitis dropped to about 1 out of 10.

Hib meningitis: As researchers became more knowledgeable about meningitis antiserums, they developed an antiserum for Hib in 1937. The combined use of antiserum given into the spinal canal and into the veins at the same time dropped the death rate for *H. influenzae* meningitis to 85 percent. While that is still an extremely high death rate, nearly everyone with Hib meningitis died before the use of Hib antiserum.

In 1944, the death rate for Hib meningitis fell dramati-

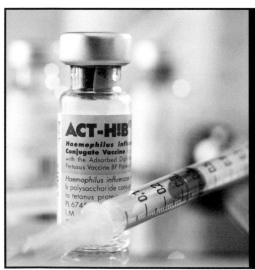

This Hib vaccine protects against Hib meningitis. This version of the vaccine is meant for children under one year of age. It also protects against diptheria and tetanus.

cally to 22 percent when doctors started using sulfa drugs (one of the first antibiotics) along with intravenous rabbit antiserum. By the early 1950s, the fatality for Hib meningitis fell even further when two antibiotics were given together, making the use of antiserum unnecessary.

Pneumococcal meningitis: The antiserums and sulfa medications were never as effective for pneumococcal disease as they had been for Hib and meningococcal meningitis. It was not until penicillin came into wide use in the late 1940s that the death rate for pneumococcal disease began to fall. When penicillin was administered into the spine and given intravenously at the same time, about 50 percent of people with pneumococcal disease lived.

MODERN TREATMENTS

Fortunately, modern antibiotics are much more effective at preventing death from all kinds of bacterial meningitis. If an ER doctor suspects bacterial meningitis, he will usually start intravenous antibiotics even before performing the spinal tap. If the patient has viral meningitis, the antibiotics won't make a difference. But if the patient has bacterial meningitis, prompt administration of antibiotics can lessen the severity of the disease or even save the patient's life. Even a few extra minutes of antibiotics can make a big difference. A suspicion of bacterial meningitis is one of the few times it is a good idea to give antibiotics first and ask questions later.

Broad-spectrum antibiotics—those that can kill several kinds of bacteria—are used at first. Once the lab identifies which bacterium is to blame for the meningitis, the doctor will begin using an antibiotic specific to that bacterium. Antibiotics commonly used in the treatment of bacterial meningitis include vancomycin, usually given in combination with ceftriaxone, cefotaxime, or ceftazidime. However, pneumococcal bacteria are getting harder and harder to kill, although widespread vaccination may be reversing that trend.

After receiving the initial dose of antibiotics, patients with bacterial meningitis are placed in ICUs. In the ICU, they receive constant attention and specialized care from nurses and doctors. Children are placed in a pediatric ICU, and newborns will be placed in the NICU. These patients are very, very sick. They will receive fluids to keep them from becoming dehydrated, and numerous intravenous medications, including antibiotics to kill the bacteria and steroids to reduce swelling of the brain and meninges.

Doctors also prescribe medications to relieve pain, to prevent seizures, and to support weakened hearts. People whose kidneys are failing may have to receive dialysis treatments (in which a patient's blood is passed through a machine to clean it). A medication called Xigris can be given to patients with septicemia. The medication is dripped into the patient's veins for 96 hours to help fight the high mortality rate of septicemia.

Bacterial meningitis patients may need a tube inserted into their throats to connect them to ventilators to help them breathe. Another tube is inserted into the bladder to collect and measure urine. A feeding tube is used if the person is unable to eat or drink. When a patient's fever soars, a cooling blanket—a blanket filled with circulating cool water—can be used to help bring down the patient's temperature. Tubes may also be placed into the brain to measure pressure of the CSF and into an artery to closely monitor blood pressure.

Patients who fall into a coma because of increased pressure in the brain are gravely ill and need especially close monitoring. Doctors often use the Glasgow Coma Scale to evaluate people who have an altered level of consciousness caused by meningitis or septicemia. The lower the numbers on the scale, the lower the chance of recovery.

Sometimes doctors put patients into medically induced

comas by giving them medications that put them to sleep, much as if they were having an operation. This medical coma state keeps the patient more comfortable during what can be a painful and terrifying time. It also helps to relieve pressure on the brain.

Factors that increase the risk of death from bacterial meningitis include:

- A delay in starting the appropriate treatment— that is, antibiotics
- A decreased level of consciousness on admission
- The onset of seizures within 24 hours of admission
- An increased pressure inside the brain
- Age—that is, infancy and older than 50
- Presence of septicemia along with the meningitis
- The need for a ventilator to support breathing

Most cases of meningitis are caused by viruses, and most of those cases are much less serious than bacterial meningitis. There is no specific treatment for viral meningitis, except for those rare cases caused by herpes virus, cytomegalovirus, or HIV. The antiviral medication acyclovir may be used for herpes meningitis. Ganciclovir may be used for severe cases of meningitis caused by cytomegalovirus. People with HIV infection are likely to be on a number of medications designed to fight the virus wherever it is, including in the CSF.

People with viral meningitis will sometimes be sent home with instructions to rest for several days in a dark, quiet room. They will take over-the-counter medications for fever and headache, and they will need to drink fluids. Caregivers—parents, a spouse, or close friends—must watch for any new symptoms, such as increased vomiting, worsening fever or headache, seizures, or changes in the level of consciousness. A follow-up visit to a doctor within a couple of days is generally recommended.

GLASGOW COMA SCALE

The Glasgow Coma Scale (GCS) is used to judge how sick people are when they have meningitis or other serious diseases or injuries that can cause coma (such as strokes, head injuries, or drug overdoses). The best response in each category is used to calculate the total number on the GCS. A GCS score of 13 to 15 indicates mild brain injury; a GCS score of 9 to 12 indicates moderate injury; a GCS of 8 or less indicates severe injury with less chance for a good recovery.

Eye Opening Response
- Spontaneously opens eyes and blinks—4 points
- Opens eyes to verbal command—3 points
- Opens eyes only to pain—2 points
- Doesn't open eyes at all—1 point

Verbal Response
- Oriented, knows name, date, place—5 points
- Confused, but can answer simple questions—4 points
- Says inappropriate words, doesn't make any sense—3 points
- Mutters, mumbles, can't understand most words people say—2 points
- No speech at all—1 point

Motor Response
- Obeys commands to move, for example, to lift arm—6 points
- Purposeful movement to pain, for example, if pinched, pushes doctor's hand away—5 points

- Withdraws or turns away from pain—4 points
- Draws arms inward to chest in response to pain (a movement seen only with moderate to severe brain injury)—3 points
- Stretches arms downward in response to pain (a movement seen only with severe brain injury)—2 points
- No response to pain—1 point

The next morning, the ER doctor spoke to Joshua's mom about sending him home. The doctor said that Joshua had viral meningitis and that there was no specific treatment for it. He advised her that Joshua should get a lot of rest in a quiet, dark room and should take acetaminophen for headache and fever. Joshua was to stay home from school for a week or so. His mom needed to watch him for a rash, confusion, or an increase in fever. If any of those symptoms occurred, she was to bring him back to the ER. Also, Joshua needed to see his family doctor the next day for a follow-up exam. Joshua had heard about meningococcal meningitis at school, and even though he still felt pretty bad, he felt lucky that he didn't have it.

While bacterial meningitis is relatively uncommon in the United States, it attracts a lot of attention because many of its victims are children, teens, and young people who are just starting out in life. One day soon, bacterial meningitis may become exceedingly rare. Read about promising new research on vaccines and medications in the next chapter.

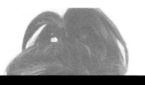

Chapter 7

WHAT'S NEW WITH MENINGITIS?

The Pig Farmer's Story

You've probably heard a lot about bird flu, but do you know about pig meningitis? In March 2006, several East Coast newspapers carried the story of a fifty-nine-year-old pig farmer from New York. The man had checked into a hospital complaining of a sudden fever, a racing heart, heavy breathing, and confusion. Doctors suspected bacterial meningitis and began antibiotics. The pig farmer made a full recovery and went home in a few days.

Doctors were surprised to discover a bacterium known as Streptococcus suis *in the man's CSF. In the United States, this bacteria had been found only in pigs, although it is becoming an increasingly common cause of human meningitis in other parts of the world. S. suis was responsible for an outbreak of pig meningitis among humans in Southeast Asia in 2005. The outbreak sickened more than 200 people and killed 38. S.* suis *is now the third most common cause of bacterial meningitis in Hong Kong.*

While isolated cases of pig meningitis in humans have occurred in Europe, the New York pig farmer was the first known case in the United States. Doctors said the public should not be concerned, but people who work with live pigs and raw pork products (such as butchers) should be on the lookout for symptoms of illness.

Much of the research on meningitis over the past few years has been focused on developing new and improved vaccines to prevent it. There have been some remarkable successes, such as the Hib vaccine that slashed meningitis caused by *H. influenzae* by 99 percent since the late 1980s. Yet better vaccines are needed for the other causes of bacterial meningitis.

For example, the two vaccines approved in the United States for the prevention of meningococcal disease fail to protect against type B, which is responsible for about one-quarter of all cases in this country. A vaccine for type B is given in New Zealand, but it has not been approved for use in the United States. Three U.S. studies are under way on vaccines for type B meningococcal disease. The trials will take several years to complete.

The pharmaceutical company Novartis is sponsoring one of the trials. The Novartis trial is testing an experimental meningococcal vaccine in young people eleven to eighteen years old. The trial started in February 2006.

The pharmaceutical company Wyeth started its trial of an experimental meningococcal vaccine in March 2006. This vaccine is for adults eighteen to twenty-five years old.

The U.S. Army Office of the Surgeon General is also sponsoring a trial. This trial involves an experimental meningococcal vaccine among adults eighteen to forty-five years old. The trial completed its first phase in November 2006.

European researchers are also looking for ways to prevent meningitis caused by type B meningococcus. In the United Kingdom, researchers are developing a vaccine that can be sprayed into the nose. Scientists know that meningococcal bacteria often live in the nose and throat of healthy people. They believe that this experimental vaccine might somehow produce a better immune response than that obtained by injected vaccines. The nasal vaccine will be tested first on adults, then on adolescents.

Scientists have discovered that some strains of type B meningococcus bacteria don't appear to make people sick. A study is under way in France to determine the genetic differences between the type B strains. In the Netherlands, researchers are using genetic techniques to create special mice which have cells in their noses and throats that are similar to those found in humans. The scientists will then use these mice to figure out exactly how and why meningococcus infects some people but not others.

Remember that Prevnar—the vaccine used to prevent pneumococcal disease in babies and toddlers—only protects against seven of the ninety known strains of the bacteria. Between 3,000 and 6,000 people each year still get pneumococcal meningitis (and many other infections caused by the same bacteria as well). A vaccine to protect against additional strains will help thousands of people. Researchers are developing vaccines that can prevent up to thirteen strains of pneumococcal disease in children under two years old.

West Nile virus has become an emerging cause of viral meningitis in the United States since the virus first arrived in 1999. Clinical trials on three slightly different vaccines started in May 2006. At present the vaccines are being tested only among adults between eighteen and seventy-five years old. While early results look promising, it remains to

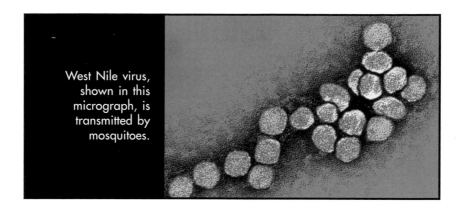

West Nile virus, shown in this micrograph, is transmitted by mosquitoes.

be seen if any of the vaccines will be recommended for widespread use to prevent meningitis and other neurological complications caused by West Nile infection.

FASTER TESTS, BETTER TREATMENTS

It's important for a doctor to know as soon as possible if a patient has bacterial meningitis, viral meningitis, or another illness. Using current laboratory methods, tests on blood and spinal fluid may take hours or even days to complete. This means that precious time could be lost before the correct treatment is started.

Testing

Newer tests that are faster and more accurate are quickly becoming available. In March 2007, the FDA approved a device that tests for the presence of genetic material in the CSF. The test, called the Xpert EV Test, distinguishes between viral and bacterial meningitis in less than three hours.

In an experiment involving other new tests, doctors tested the CSF of twelve patients with bacterial meningitis, eleven with viral meningitis, and twenty-seven healthy volunteers. Within thirty minutes, doctors knew whether the CSF contained bacteria or viruses, or whether it was from

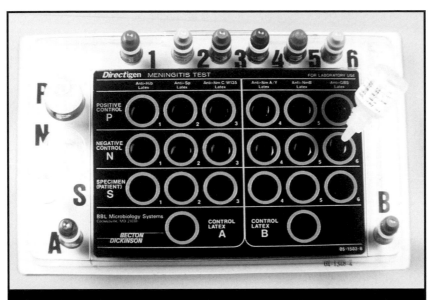

The ability to diagnose patients with meningitis quickly and accurately can save a patient from death or permanent physical damage. Diagnostic equipment such as this kit is portable and easy to use, even outside of a laboratory or hospital.

one of the healthy people. Unlike older tests, the new test was correct 100 percent of the time.

Another experimental test can identify the four major causes of bacterial meningitis—group B strep, Hib, and pneumococcal and meningococcal infections—in the CSF in only ten to fifteen minutes. With these super-fast tests, doctors can start the correct antibiotics for bacterial meningitis right away.

Antibiotics

Antibiotics help most people with bacterial meningitis. However, some strains of bacteria are becoming increasingly more resistant to these powerful medications. Scientists are constantly looking for new sources of antibiotics and they're looking in some pretty strange places! For example, chemicals that fight bacteria have been found in animals as different as frogs and moths, rabbits and sharks, and horseshoe crabs and guinea pigs.

Consider the Komodo dragon. These 200-pound holdouts from the dinosaur age live on isolated islands in Indonesia. Komodo dragon saliva is so thick with dangerous bacteria that scientists wondered why the dragons don't infect themselves. It turns out that Komodo dragon saliva contains a potent natural antibiotic. One day researchers will figure out how to develop human antibiotics from these natural animal products.

Bacteria Killers

Scientists are also looking at unusual viruses called bacteriophages to help fight bacteria. Bacteriophages prey on bacteria; in fact, the word means "bacteria eaters." Called phages for short, these viruses are only 1/40th the size of the bacteria they attack. That would be like a 2-pound mosquito tackling an 80-pound sixth grader! When a phage comes across its favorite food, whether it be pneumococcus or *E. coli*, it injects its own DNA into the bacterium.

It isn't long before the bacterium is producing new viruses instead of new bacteria. Once the bacterium is filled with viruses, it bursts, sending hundreds of new viruses off in search of the next bacterium. By the time phages finish killing off a mob of bacteria, the body's own immune system comes along and destroys the phages. Phages don't seem to be harmful to humans.

Dr. Anthony S. Fauci, director of the National Institute of Allergy and Infectious Diseases, says, "We can potentially tailor these viruses to infect and destroy bacteria that have mutated and become drug-resistant." Phages are like living antibiotics, stalking bacteria and mutating as needed to keep up with them. While phage therapy may be a few years away in the United States, the potential to use phages for antibiotic-resistant infections, including those that cause bacterial meningitis, greatly interests U.S. scientists.

CLINICAL TRIALS

A clinical trial is an investigational research study with human volunteers to find out how well new medications and treatments work. The studies can be sponsored and funded by governmental organizations (for example, the National Institutes of Health), medical institutions (such as large hospitals), health foundations (for example, the Bill & Melinda Gates Foundation), and drug companies (such as Wyeth and Novartis).

People who agree to participate in clinical trials must sign papers saying they are aware of the potential risks and the possible benefits of taking a new medication or trying a new treatment. These are the activities that occur during each phase of a clinical trial:

Phase I   Is the medication safe? Researchers test an experimental drug in a small group of people (twenty to eighty) for the first time to evaluate its safety, to determine a safe dosage range, and to identify side effects.

Phase II   Does the medication work? The experimental drug is given to a larger group of people (one hundred to three hundred) to see if it is effective and to further evaluate its safety.

Phase III   How does the new medication compare
with existing medications? The experimental drug is given to larger groups of
people (one thousand to three thousand)
to confirm its effectiveness, monitor its
side effects, compare it to commonly
used treatments, and to collect information that will allow the experimental
drug to be used safely.

Phase IV   Are there other potential uses for this
medication, and are there any long-term
adverse effects? The new drug or vaccine
is on the market, but additional information continues to be collected as more
and more people take the medication
over a longer period of time.

Because bacterial meningitis so often causes septicemia, treatment for septicemia is another area of
research. One product that offers hope is called BPI (for
bactericidal permeability increasing protein). In simple
terms, this experimental medication is similar to a protein found in normal white blood cells—the same cells
our body uses to fight off invading bacteria and other
organisms.

When large amounts of synthetic BPI are given, the
medication kills meningococcal bacteria and at the same
time, neutralizes the dangerous endotoxin the bacteria
produce. Remember that meningococcal bacteria release
huge amounts of deadly endotoxin even as antibiotics are
killing off the bacteria themselves. Endotoxin is a major

cause of organ failure and death with meningococcal meningitis. Although BPI has been given to only a few people in investigational trials, it reduced the death rate by one third in one study.

Antiviral Medication

Let's not forget viral meningitis. While it is usually less serious than bacterial meningitis, it can make people very sick—and occasionally, it may be fatal. There are not many antiviral medications for viral meningitis. The most common cause of viral meningitis is the large group of viruses called the enteroviruses. At present, there is no antiviral medication for that kind of meningitis.

A medication called pleconaril had been tested in clinical trials involving infants with severe meningitis caused by enteroviruses. However, pleconaril was withdrawn from the market in 2005 when the risk of side effects was found to be greater than the benefit. Researchers continue to look for new medications to treat viral meningitis. But it will likely take a few years before any such medications are tested and approved for widespread use.

With improved vaccines, faster tests, and better treatments, meningitis may one day become a disease of the past, a disease that seldom strikes citizens of developed nations such as our own. Yet can we really declare victory over meningitis when it continues to kill thousands and sicken hundreds of thousands of people in developing countries each year? Bill Gates, the billionaire brain behind Microsoft, doesn't think so.

The Bill & Melinda Gates Foundation has given millions of dollars to fund a global partnership that is developing an effective and affordable new vaccine to prevent type A meningococcal meningitis. Type A is rare in the United States, so U.S. drug companies have little motivation to make a vaccine for that strain. Yet type A is the leading cause of meningococcal meningitis in Africa's meningitis belt. The goal of the Gates partnership is to vaccinate every African between one and twenty-nine years of age against type A meningococcal meningitis over the next decade or so.

It's tragic when people die of an infectious disease such as meningitis, especially if they arc children or young adults with their entire lives ahead of them. And health-care providers are frustrated that meningitis is still killing and maiming people, despite the fact that the disease is often both preventable and treatable. There's a lot of good news about meningitis right now. Yet there's still a very long way to go before the world's children are safe from this terrible illness.

GLOSSARY

amoeba: single-cell organisms considered to be the most primitive form of animal life. Some amoeba may cause disease in humans.

antibiotics: medications used to fight infections caused by bacteria (and some parasites such as malaria). Antibiotics do not kill viruses.

antibodies: proteins produced in the body as an immune response to help defend against invading foreign substances such as viruses and bacteria

antiserum: serum from an animal that has developed antibodies to a particular bacterium. An antiserum is injected into a human to help protect the person from that disease. Meningitis antiserums were used on people during the early part of the twentieth century.

arachnoid: the middle layer of the meninges that looks somewhat like a spider web

bacteria: microscopic organisms that eat, excrete, and reproduce on their own. They live everywhere. Some are harmless, while others may cause serious disease.

bacteriophage: viruses that can invade bacteria. They may one day be used like antibiotics to help fight bacterial meningitis and other bacterial diseases.

booster shots: extra doses of vaccines given after the initial series to help maintain immunity. For example, lifelong periodic tetanus booster shots are recommended.

carrier: a healthy person who carries bacteria, such as the ones that cause meningitis, without becoming ill

Centers for Disease Control and Prevention (CDC): the U.S. agency responsible for monitoring and tracking diseases. Among other activities, the CDC is charged with protecting the health and safety of Americans.

cerebrospinal fluid (CSF): the fluid produced in the brain that circulates through the meninges and spinal canal. Its purpose is to cushion and protect the brain and spinal cord.

clinical trial: a research study in human volunteers to find out if new medications and treatments are both safe and effective

colonized: when bacteria live in or on healthy people without making them sick, the people are said to be colonized with the bacteria

coma: the loss of consciousness due to brain injury. People in comas are not able to eat, talk, or to move with purpose, although they may show some involuntary movements.

contagious: an infectious disease that can be transmitted from one person to another. For example, colds and flu are highly contagious.

cranial nerves: the twelve pairs of nerves that control the movement and sensations of the head and face. These nerves arise from the brain and may be damaged by meningitis, leaving victims with loss of hearing or sight.

Cryptococcus neoformans: a fungus commonly found in

soil and bird droppings. It may cause meningitis in people with weakened immune systems.

CT scan: sometimes called a CAT scan (for computerized axial tomography). This medical test produces images of cross-sections of the brain or other body parts. The images can help to identify problems that cannot be seen on regular X-rays.

dura mater: the outermost of the meninges. The dura mater is a strong membrane that lines the inside of the skull and continues down the spinal cord.

endotoxin: a type of poison released by some kinds of bacteria, such as meningococcus. Endotoxins can weaken the heart and cause bleeding into the skin and internal organs.

enteroviruses: a large group of viruses that normally live in the gastrointestinal and respiratory tracts. Viruses in this group are the most common cause of viral meningitis.

Escherichia coli (E. coli): a common bacterium that can cause meningitis and other diseases in babies, the elderly, and people with weak immune systems

flagella: tail-like projections on bacteria that propel them

flaviviruses: viruses carried by mosquitoes that can cause meningitis or encephalitis, such as the West Nile virus

fungus: a plantlike microorganism that may cause disease. It includes infections such as ringworm and athletes' foot

group B streptococcus: the bacterium *Streptococcus*

agalactiae that can cause meningitis in newborns. Infants are infected as they pass through the birth canal.

Haemophilus influenzae type B (Hib): a bacterium that can cause meningitis. While Hib was once the most common cause of meningitis in children, vaccines have nearly eliminated it in North America.

herd immunity: the theory that a population of humans or animals is protected against a given disease if most of the population has been vaccinated against it

Herpes simplex viruses: viruses that cause cold sores and genital herpes. They are the second most common cause of viral meningitis after enteroviruses.

immune system: the parts of the body that work together to identify and fight disease-causing organisms such as bacteria and viruses

invasive disease: illness caused by bacteria entering normally sterile parts of the body, such as cerebrospinal fluid and blood

Listeria monocytogenes: a bacterium found in soil, water, the gastrointestinal tract, and in tainted food. Listeria can cause meningitis in newborns, infants, pregnant women, and the elderly.

meninges: the three thin membranes that protect the brain and spinal cord

meningitis: an infection of the meninges and the CSF

meningitis belt: the region of Africa stretching across the continent where epidemics of bacterial meningitis regularly occur

meningococcal disease: the common term for diseases, including meningitis, caused by the bacterium *Neisseria meningitidis*

microorganisms: living organisms so small that you need a microscope to see them. Bacteria, viruses, and fungi are microoganisms.

Naegleria fowleri: an amoeba found around the world in warm freshwater that can cause an especially deadly type of meningitis

Neisseria meningitidis: a bacterium that can cause meningitis and the only one known to cause widespread outbreaks of meningitis

pia mater: the innermost meninges that clings to the brain and spinal cord

pili: tiny, hairlike projections on some species of bacteria that allow the bacteria to attach to cells. Once attached, bacteria can more easily enter the cell to cause disease.

pneumococcal disease: the common term for diseases, including meningitis, caused by the bacterium *Streptococcus pneumoniae*

prokaryotes: microorganisms whose cells have no nucleus. Instead, the DNA material in prokaryotes floats freely within the cell walls.

seizure: an electrical disturbance in the brain that can cause severe and involuntary muscular contractions. Seizures may involve just one part of the body, such as an arm, or they may involve the whole body and lead to unconsciousness.

septicemia: a disease caused by large numbers of bacteria circulating in the blood

serotype: a group of specifically related microorganisms such as bacteria. Minor differences in the sugary coating of bacteria can make some serotypes more dangerous than others.

serum: the clear, yellowish liquid part of the blood left when the red blood cells, white blood cells, and platelets have been removed. Serum contains antibodies.

sickle-cell disease: an inherited disorder in which red blood cells form half-moon shapes instead of being round. People with sickle-cell disease are at high risk for many infections, including bacterial meningitis.

spinal canal: the passageway formed by the vertebra (the bones of the spine) that surrounds and protects the spinal cord and meninges

spinal cord: a column of nerves that runs from the bottom of the brain down through the spinal canal. All nerves in the body except the cranial nerves originate in the spinal cord. The spinal cord is wrapped in meninges.

spinal tap: the procedure in which a doctor inserts a needle between the bones of the lower spine to obtain a sample of CSF. Also called a lumbar puncture.

Staphylococcus aureus: a common bacterium often found on human skin that may cause meningitis or other infections

Streptococcus pneumoniae: a bacterium that can cause meningitis and many other diseases

subarachnoid space: the space between the pia mater and

the arachnoid layer of the meninges. The subarachnoid space is filled with cerebral spinal fluid.

vaccine: a medication that stimulates the body's production of disease-fighting antibodies against a specific organism (a bacterium or virus)

virus: a tiny infectious particle that requires a living host (a plant or animal cell) to survive and reproduce

World Health Organization (WHO): a part of the United Nations system that monitors and responds to health issues and disease outbreaks around the world

RESOURCES

Centers for Disease Control and Prevention (CDC)
1600 Clifton Road
Atlanta, GA 30333
(800) 311-3435
www.cdc.gov

The CDC's mission is to promote health and quality of life by preventing and controlling disease, injury, and disability. The CDC conducts disease research to develop methods to better identify, control, and cure diseases. It also monitors and investigates health problems around the world and in the United States. Each week it releases its Morbidity and Mortality Weekly Report (www.cdc.gov/mmwr), which tracks many health-related issues, as well as disease outbreaks.

KidsHealth
www.kidshealth.org

KidsHealth is a project of the Nemours Foundation's Center for Children's Health, an organization established in 1936 by philanthropist Alfred I. DuPont. The project is dedicated to improving the health and spirit of children. The KidsHealth website has separate areas for kids, teens, and parents about important health issues. Doctors and health-care experts review all information before it is posted on the website. Search the site for articles about meningitis.

MedlinePlus
www.medlineplus.org

MedlinePlus is an online service provided by the National Library of Medicine and the National Institutes of Health. It offers extensive health information on diseases and drugs, and the latest health news. Go to the site and search for articles about meningitis.

Meningitis Foundation of America
6610 North Shadeland Avenue
Suite 220
Indianapolis, IN 46220
(800) 668-1129
www.musa.org

The Meningitis Foundation of America supports meningitis victims and their families, educates the public and medical professionals about meningitis and early diagnosis and treatment, and supports the development of vaccines and other methods of preventing meningitis.

Meningitis Research Foundation
Midland Way, Thornbury
Bristol, BS35 2BS
England
www.meningitis.org

The Meningitis Research Foundation is a British charity that funds research to prevent meningitis and to improve survival rates and outcomes. The organization provides education to reduce death and disability and gives support to people affected by meningitis around the world. Meningitis Research Foundation's vision is a world free from meningitis.

Meningitis Vaccine Project
13, chemin du Levant
Bâtiment Avant-Centre
01210 Ferney-Voltaire
France
www.meningvax.org

The Meningitis Vaccine Project is an organization based in France. It is a partnership between the World Health Organization and the Program for Appropriate Technology in Health. Created in 2001 with funding from the Bill & Melinda Gates Foundation, its goal is to eliminate epidemic meningitis as a public health problem in Sub-Saharan Africa.

National Meningitis Association
738 Robinson Farms Drive
Marietta, GA 30068
(866) 366.3662
www.nmaus.org

The National Meningitis Association's mission is to ensure that every child in the United States is offered protection against meningococcal meningitis through vaccination programs. The association helps educate families and medical professionals about the dangers of bacterial meningitis and how to prevent it. It supports research into improved meningitis vaccines and into improved treatments for meningitis patients. The association also assists families and survivors of meningococcal meningitis.

World Health Organization (WHO)
Avenue Appia 20
1211 Geneva 27, Switzerland
www.who.int/en

Part of the United Nations, WHO's objective is the highest possible level of health for all people. The organization defines health not merely as the absence of disease but as a state of complete physical, mental, and social well-being. The website offers updated information about disease outbreaks around the world. For information about Africa's meningitis belt, go to the website and search for "Meningitis Belt."

FURTHER READING

Brynie, Faith Hickman. *101 Questions about Your Immune System*. Minneapolis: Twenty-First Century Books, 2000.

Friedlander, Mark P., Jr., and Terry Phillips. *The Immune System: Your Body's Disease Fighting Army*. Minneapolis: Twenty-First Century Books, 1998.

Friedlander, Mark P., Jr. *Outbreak: Disease Detectives at Work*. Minneapolis: Twenty-First Century Books, 2003.

Goldsmith, Connie. *Invisible Invaders: Dangerous Infectious Diseases*. Minneapolis: Twenty-First Century Books, 2006.

———. *Superbugs Strike Back: When Antibiotics Fail*. Minneapolis: Twenty-First Century Books, 2007.

Klosterman, Lorrie. *Meningitis*. Tarrytown, NY: Marshall Cavendish/Benchmark Books, 2006.

Lawton, Sandra Augustyn, ed. *Body Information for Teens: Health Tips About Maintaining Well-Being for a Lifetime*. Detroit, MI: Omnigraphics, 2007.

Reeves, Diane Lindsey. *Teen Careers in Health Science*. New York: Checkmark Books/Facts On File, 2006.

SOURCE NOTES

63 Terry Rombeck, "New Life After Near Death," *LJWorld.com*, April 24, 2005, http://www2.ljworld.com/news/2005/apr/24/new_life_after/.

65 Richard Burgess, "Meningitis Vaccination Plan Targets 6,500," *RedOrbit*, February 15, 2006, http://www.redorbit.com/news/health/393018/meningitis_vaccination_plan_targets_6500/index.html.

72 Dorsey Griffith, "Reported Side Effects Deal Blow to Meningitis Vaccine," *Sacramento Bee*, October 23, 2005.

103 "Scientists Discover Potential New Way to Control Drug-Resistant Bacteria," *NIH News*, September 23, 2004, www.nih.gov/news/pr/sep2004/niaid-22.htm.

SELECTED BIBLIOGRAPHY

Behrman, Richard E., et al. *Nelson Textbook of Pediatrics*. 16th ed. Philadelphia: WB Saunders, 2000.

Biddle, Wayne. *A Field Guide to Germs*. New York: Random House, 1995.

Bilukha, Oleg O., and Nancy Rosenstein. "Prevention and Control of Meningococcal Disease." *Morbidity and Mortality Weekly Report* 54, RR07 (2005): 1-21. Available online at http://www.cdc.gov/mmwr/preview/mmwrhtml/rr5407a1.htm.

Centers for Disease Control and Prevention. "Viral (Aseptic) Meningitis." http://www.cdc.gov/ncidod/dvrd/revb/enterovirus/viral_meningitis.htm, 2005.

————. *Epidemiology & Prevention of Vaccine-Preventable Diseases*. 10th ed. (2007). Available online at http://www.cdc.gov/nip/publications/pink/def_pink_full.htm.

"Enhanced Surveillance of Epidemic Meningococcal Meningitis in Africa: A Three-Year Experience." World Health Organization's *Weekly Epidemiological Record* 80, no. 37 (September 16, 2005): 313-320. http://www.who.int/wer/2005/wer8037.pdf.

Heymann, David L., ed. *Control of Communicable Diseases Manual*. 18th ed. Washington, DC: American Public Health Association, 2004.

Institute of Medicine. *Microbial Threats to Health: Emergence, Detection, and Response*. Washington: National Academies Press, 2003.

"Killer disease on campus." *Nova* (Public Broadcasting System, September 3, 2002), produced by Jeremy Llewellyn-Jones. http://www.pbs.org/wgbh/nova/meningitis/.

Kyaw, Moe H., et al. "Effect of Introduction of the Pneumococcal Conjugate Vaccine on Drug-Resistant *Streptococcus pneumoniae*." *New England Journal of Medicine* 354, no. 14 (2006): 1455–1463.

Lohsl, Connie, and Catherine Spader. "Meningitis: A New Vaccine Brings Hopes for Old Fears." *NurseWeek* 18, no. 22 (2005): 14–15.

Meningitis Foundation of America. "Frequently Asked Questions." http://www.musa.org/pdfs/mfa_brochure.pdf, 2006.

Meningitis Research Foundation. "Research." http://www.meningitis. org/research, 2007.

Murray, Patrick R., Ken S. Rosenthal, and Michael A. Pfaller. *Medical Microbiology*. 5th ed. Philadelphia: Mosby Elsevier, 2005.

National Meningitis Association. "Backgrounder: Meningococcal Disease in Adolescents and Young Adults." http://www.nmaus.org/ press_room/downloads/Adolescent_Backgrounder.pdf, 2006.

Poehling, Katherine A., et al. "Invasive Pneumococcal Disease Among Infants Before and After Introduction of Pneumococcal Conjugate Vaccine." *Journal of the American Medical Association* 295, no. 14 (2006): 1668–1674.

"Rapid Meningitis Tests Provide Fast Answers in Emergency Situations." *Medical News Today*, July 1, 2005. http://www.medicalnewstoday. com/medicalnews.php?newsid=26786.

Shnayerson, Michael, and Mark J. Plotkin. *The Killers Within: The Deadly Rise of Drug-Resistant Bacteria*. Boston: Little, Brown, 2002.

Swartz, Morton N. "History of Medicine: On Bacterial Meningitis." *New England Journal of Medicine* 351, no. 18: 1826–1828.

Thompson, M.J., et al. "Clinical Recognition of Meningococcal Disease in Children and Adolescents." *The Lancet* 367, no. 9508 (2006): 397–403.

Tully, Joanna, et al. "Risk and Protective Factors for Meningococcal Disease in Adolescents: Matched Cohort Study." *British Medical Journal* 332, no. 7539 (2006): 445–450.

U.S. Army Center for Health Promotion and Preventive Medicine. "Meningococcal Vaccine: What You Need to Know." http://www. vaccines.mil/documents/290meningdmis.pdf, 2001.

Van de Beek, Diederik, et al. "Community-Acquired Bacterial Meningitis in Adults." *New England Journal of Medicine* 354, no. 1 (2006): 44–53.

Willett, E. *Meningitis*. Berkeley Heights, NJ: Enslow Publishers, 1999.

World Health Organization. Fact sheet no. 41: "Meningococcal meningitis" (May 2003) http://www.who.int/mediacentre/factsheets/fs141/en/print.html.

DNA (deoxyribonucleic acid), 25
dormitory living, 46–47
DTaP/Hib vaccine, 68
dura mater, 21

EEGs (electroencephalograms), 90
elderly, vaccinations for, 74
Elise, 36–37, 40–41
endotoxin damage, 59–63, 105–106
enteroviruses, 32, 33, 34, 40, 47
Escherichia coli, 30, 32, 40

facial nerve, 22
fever, 85
flaviviruses, 33, 34
Flexner, Simon, 91–92

GBS. See *Streptococcus agalactiae* (group B strep, GBS)
Glasgow Coma Scale (GCS), 96–97
glossopharyngeal nerve, 22
Goya, Francisco de, 12
Guillain-Barré syndrome, 71–72

Haemophilus influenzae type B (Hib): about, 29, 32, 43; antiserums, 92; vaccines for, 68–69, 99–100
hajj pilgrimage, 17
hand washing, 79–80
heart, damage to, 59–60
herd immunity, 76
herpes viruses, 33, 34, 40
herpes zoster virus, 40
Hib. See *Haemophilus influenzae* type B (Hib)
HIV, 33

hypoglossal nerve, 22

immune system: about, 65–66; strength, 37, 53
infants and children: onset, 43–45; risks and causes, 41–43; susceptibility, 12–13; vaccinations, 68–69, 70, 76, 78; worldwide infection rates, 14–15
infectious diseases, in world, 14–17
inflammatory response, 56–57
influenza, 33
International Travel and Health (WHO), 19

Jack, 20–21, 30–31
Jenner, Edward, 65
Jochmann, G., 91
Joshua, 82, 88, 90–91, 97

Keller, Helen, 10–11
kidney dialysis, 94
KidsHealth, 115
Klebsiella pneumoniae, 30
Komodo dragon saliva, 103

light sensitivity, 86
Listeria monocytogenes (Listeria), 30, 32, 48

manometer, 89
Marso, Andy, 50–51, 55, 61, 62–63, 73–74
McCormick, Joe, 18
measles virus, 33
MedlinePlus, 115
Meigs, Leslie, 87
Menactra vaccine, 70–71
meninges: defined, 21; normal vs. inflamed, 24
meningitis, bacterial: in adults,

ABOUT THE AUTHOR

Connie Goldsmith is a registered nurse with a bachelor of science degree in nursing and a master of public administration degree in health care. She is the author of *Influenza, Invisible Invaders: Dangerous Infectious Diseases, Superbugs Strike Back: When Antibiotics Fail,* and *Lost in Death Valley.* She has also published more than two hundred magazine articles, mostly on health topic for adults and children. She lives near Sacramento, California.